Mastering Microsoft Teams

End User Guide to Practical Usage, Collaboration, and Governance

Melissa Hubbard
Matthew J. Bailey

Apress®

Mastering Microsoft Teams

Melissa Hubbard
Withum Digital, Bethesda, Maryland, USA

Matthew J. Bailey
Noteworthy Technology Inc., Falls Church, Virginia, USA

ISBN-13 (pbk): 978-1-4842-3669-7
https://doi.org/10.1007/978-1-4842-3670-3

ISBN-13 (electronic): 978-1-4842-3670-3

Library of Congress Control Number: 2018954050

Managing Director, Apress Media LLC: Welmoed Spahr
Acquisitions Editor: Joan Murray
Development Editor: Laura Berendson
Coordinating Editor: Jill Balzano

Cover designed by eStudioCalamar

Cover image designed by Freepik (www.freepik.com)

Distributed to the book trade worldwide by Springer Science+Business Media New York, 233 Spring Street, 6th Floor, New York, NY 10013. Phone 1-800-SPRINGER, fax (201) 348-4505, e-mail orders-ny@springer-sbm.com, or visit www.springeronline.com. Apress Media, LLC is a California LLC and the sole member (owner) is Springer Science + Business Media Finance Inc (SSBM Finance Inc). SSBM Finance Inc is a **Delaware** corporation.

For information on translations, please e-mail rights@apress.com, or visit http://www.apress.com/rights-permissions.

Apress titles may be purchased in bulk for academic, corporate, or promotional use. eBook versions and licenses are also available for most titles. For more information, reference our Print and eBook Bulk Sales web page at http://www.apress.com/bulk-sales.

Any source code or other supplementary material referenced by the author in this book is available to readers on GitHub via the book's product page, located at www.apress.com/9781484236697. For more detailed information, please visit http://www.apress.com/source-code.

Printed on acid-free paper

Melissa's Dedication
This book is dedicated to my daughter, Catherine.

Matthew's Dedication
This book is dedicated to underprivileged and homeless gay youth seeking a better life via a career in technology.

Table of Contents

About the Authors

Melissa Hubbard is a Microsoft MVP and an Office 365 and SharePoint consultant specializing in collaboration solutions and automating business processes. She is a certified Project Management Professional (PMP) experienced in project management and quality assurance as well as implementing SharePoint and Office 365 solutions. She is passionate about user adoption, governance, and training. Melissa regularly blogs and speaks at events and conferences, most recently on the topics of Microsoft Teams and Flow.

Matthew J. Bailey is a Microsoft MVP in Office Server and Services and a Microsoft Certified Trainer (MCT) for Noteworthy Technology Training, specializing in SharePoint, Office 365 (including Teams), Azure, and Power BI. Combining his consulting expertise with major corporations and his technical knowledge of SharePoint and other Microsoft technologies, he solves business challenges. Matthew is a highly regarded presenter at conferences, such as Ignite, technical events, and user groups. He holds his MCSE, MCP, and MCSA and is an avid blogger and author, most recently of *The SharePoint Business Analyst Guide* (independently published, 2017).

About the Technical Reviewer

 **Erica Toelle** has been an internationally recognized speaker on Enterprise Content Management and Compliance focused on SharePoint and Office 365 since 2004. She fell in love with Microsoft Teams as a participant in the pre-release beta and has provided leadership on multiple Microsoft Teams deployments.

As the Product Evangelist at RecordPoint, she shares best practices along with real-world experiences through conferences, workshops, webinars, and online publications. Erica is a sought-after expert, and has been hired by more than 50 Fortune 500 companies, including Microsoft's SharePoint and Microsoft Teams product groups, and Microsoft IT.

Introduction

Microsoft Teams is the heart of collaboration and communication within Office 365, integrating many applications and services all in one platform. The virtual workspace provided by Microsoft Teams offers a plethora of time-saving and efficiency features that organizations of all sizes can benefit from. Since Microsoft Teams is such a new application, the story is still being written on the value realized by implementation and adoption. In order for organizations to fully appreciate Microsoft Teams, end users must be fully adept in how to use the features. Moreover, business owners must understand how to provide training, governance, and drive user adoption of Microsoft Teams. In this book, all of these scenarios are addressed.

Mastering Microsoft Teams is for anyone that is planning to begin using Microsoft Teams, as well as anyone that has already been using Microsoft Teams but wants to learn more. Additionally, business owners, project managers, and IT decision makers will benefit from Mastering Microsoft Teams, as management, governance, user adoption, and training are examined at length.

The layout of the book begins by answering what Microsoft Teams is, followed by chapters on how to work, communicate, and hold meetings in Teams. These chapters provide step-by-step guidance on how to perform different actions, as well as tips and tricks to help you get the most out of the application. The next chapters focus on user adoption and governance. These are very important chapters for IT decision makers and business owners, but all Microsoft Teams users will benefit from gaining insight on how to best manage and plan for Microsoft Teams.

Microsoft Teams is continously updated with additional functionality. Depending on when you are reading this book, we acknowledge that many things may have changed already. The final chapter discusses known issues with and the limitations of Microsoft Teams, as well as what is planned for the future.

CHAPTER 1

Introduction to Microsoft Teams

If you are reading this book, it is highly likely that you have heard some of the excitement surrounding Microsoft Teams. Understanding the value of the application and knowing about its components and how they interact with each other is a good way to start learning about the product. In this chapter, we explain the different methods of accessing Microsoft Teams and the different features that combine to make it work. If you're ready to begin your journey of learning Microsoft Teams, without further ado, let's begin!

In today's working world, we all struggle with being on a short schedule, trying to connect with remote workers, and getting our job tasks completed on time. Often there are many people required to work on the same information or documents to accomplish a task. People's work is spread across multiple locations, making it time-consuming and confusing to multitask. These business problems can be resolved with Microsoft Teams.

Chat, meetings, video and voice calls, document collaboration, file storage and sharing, retrieving information, notes, third-party tool integration, and more have been combined into a hub for teamwork into the Microsoft Teams platform. Microsoft Teams can be thought of as one "super application" that integrates many different apps into one program so that you don't have to open and connect to many apps separately.

Our favorite description of the product is this: "If someone put Skype for Business/ Skype, Outlook's meetings and mailbox, Office 365 Groups, a persistent chat client, Word/Excel/PowerPoint, OneDrive for Business, a SharePoint site collection, and Azure Active Directory (AAD), then mixed them together and cooked them in the oven, Microsoft Teams would pop out." You can then "season to taste" by adding countless different other apps from Office 365 or outside companies to make a recipe of your own.

© Melissa Hubbard, Matthew J. Bailey 2018
M. Hubbard and M. J. Bailey, *Mastering Microsoft Teams*, https://doi.org/10.1007/978-1-4842-3670-3_1

Examples of other Microsoft apps you can add to a team are Microsoft Planner for project management, Visual Studio Team Services for developer teams, a specific SharePoint site for storage or collaboration, Power BI for data visualization, PowerApps for semicomplex form creation, Stream for video, or Forms for simple data collection. Some examples of non-Microsoft apps that you could add include GitHub for developer's code, Jira for project management, Adobe Sign for electronic signature collection, and Hootsuite for social media monitoring.

Although Chapter 5 goes into more about real-world use cases for Microsoft Teams, Figures 1-1 and 1-2 show how to set up and use a team. First, let's start with what a new, blank team looks like.

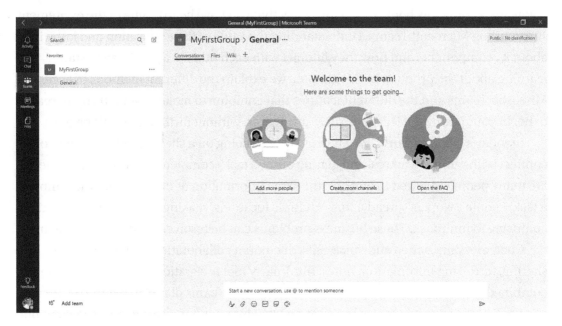

Figure 1-1. *A brand-new empty team*

As you can see in Figure 1-1, there is not too much happening in a new team. Think of it as an empty "virtual office" waiting to be filled with other co-workers or associates, discussions, files, projects, and video calls. Microsoft Teams is a part of Microsoft's *modern workplace,* a vision that allows distributed people to work together in a digital, flexible workspace.

As an example of what a team can look like in production, Figure 1-2 is a quick screen shot of a team used for a new product launch. The team has added channels, tabs, applications such as Adobe Sign and Power BI, files, meetings, chats, and many of the other things that a team uses while working on a project. But don't be overwhelmed! There is a lot to learn as you make your journey through this book. Showing you what is possible helps you get excited in learning it! Figure 1-2 shows what an active team with lots of activity looks like.

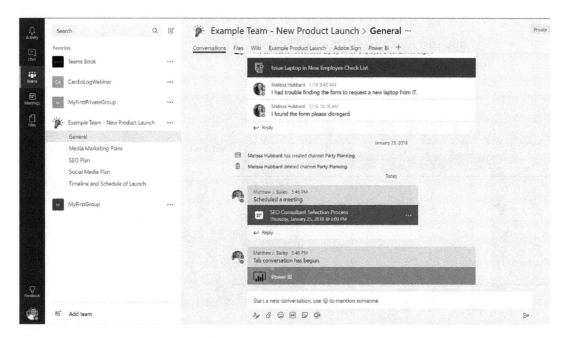

Figure 1-2. *An example team for a new product launch with lots of activity and interaction*

Microsoft Teams is very fluid and can be used for many different purposes. A team working on a new product launch, a group of people working to develop and launch a small software product, or even authors collaborating to write a book are just a few of examples of why people might use Microsoft Teams.

Having a goal of how you like to work, what you want to work on, and who you want to work with should be a part of every team's setup process. We review these topics in more depth in upcoming chapters.

How to Use and Access Teams

As you see in Figure 1-3, Teams is accessible via three different methods. Each format that you access a team in places slightly different parameters around what you can do with it. As an example, you currently have the option to access a team through the following ways:

- Your Internet browser by accessing your Office 365 tenant

- The Teams client application installed on a Windows-based computer

- The app installed on either an iOS-based (Apple) or an Android-based smartphone

Figure 1-3. *Teams is available as an installed client for Windows or Mac computers, as an app for iPhones, Android phones, or Windows phones, and via some web browsers.*

What you will probably notice first is that based on which type of client you are accessing, you have different features available to you. In the case of the Internet site or Windows client vs. the smartphone app, this is pretty much an industry standard. Most phone apps are not quite able to provide as much functionality as the other ways an application might be created. For the most part, enough features exist on all platforms to use the product successfully. Just be aware that the product has variances, and because it is new to the market, will continue to have many features being added, changed, or updated on its different clients.

Background: The Journey from Skype

Teams was built by the Skype for Business product group at Microsoft. Skype for Business will eventually become Microsoft Teams, however, it is important to note that this is a longer-term vision and not something that will happen immediately. At the moment, there is still a Skype for Business 2019 version planned to rollout that will be supported for many years. At the moment, Microsoft Teams is *only* available in the cloud; it is not available to be installed on local servers. Although Teams works with an on-premises installation of Microsoft Exchange (one of the pieces of Teams), it is important to note that currently some of the features, such as eDiscovery for Teams, will not work in that scenario.

As a quick point of reference, to utilize all the functionality that Teams has available and the new features continually being added, you need to be fully in the cloud on the Office 365 suite and all the related applications (SharePoint, Exchange, Skype for Business, and OneDrive for Business).

It is also important to note that although Microsoft Teams is built in part from Skype for Business, not all the features from Skype for Business are available in Teams at the moment. According to the Microsoft roadmap, however, they are in progress and should be delivered in the near future (or have already been delivered, depending upon when you are reading this book).

What Is Included When Creating a Team

Microsoft Teams is a combination of different applications rolled into one. However, there are some key ingredients that allow Teams to function. Each time you create a new team, the following items are created in the background on Microsoft's servers outside of Teams:

- Office 365 Groups (Modern Groups)—unless you choose an existing group when you add a team

- SharePoint site collection (with a document library)

- Exchange Online group mailbox

When you are using Microsoft Teams, it might not be immediately apparent that you are using these other pieces of software because they are "masked" behind the Microsoft Teams interface. One example of this is the Files tab in your team. In Figure 1-4, you can see that your documents all appear to be in Teams. However, they are really stored in SharePoint behind the scenes. We have elaborated this in Figure 1-4, which is similar to the meetings that are stored in Outlook. As a regular user, this isn't extremely important to know; however, if you are the administrator of a Microsoft Teams environment, these are key notes you want to be aware of because some of the maintenance and repairs that you perform might be done directly in that software, and not via Microsoft Teams.

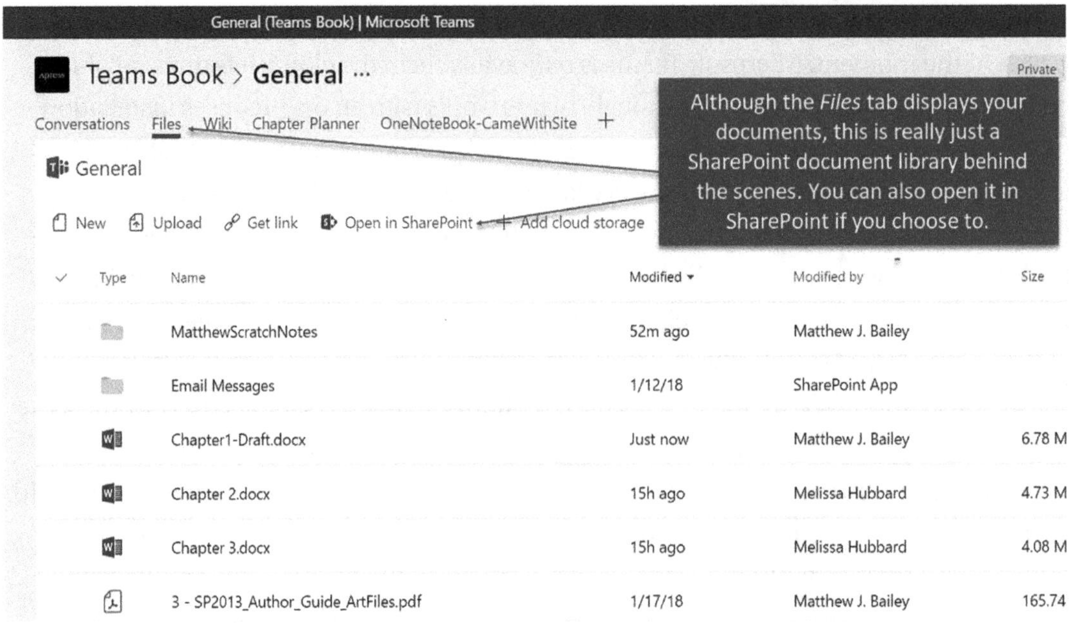

Figure 1-4. *An example of how the Microsoft Teams interface surfaces data from other applications so that it "appears" as though it is all in one place*

SharePoint and Teams

When creating a team, one of the components it creates is a Modern SharePoint Online site with a document library. SharePoint Online must be active in your tenant to work with Microsoft Teams, because SharePoint On-Premises is not supported. The Shared Documents library is created inside this team for you; however, there are ways to use an existing document library from another SharePoint site if you currently have all of your documents somewhere else.

Note   Although each channel in Microsoft Teams has a corresponding folder in SharePoint Online for the files that you work with, the folder is not created until there is actually a file uploaded.

Some of the files that users upload are stored "behind the scenes" in this SharePoint document library. Figure 1-5 shows a SharePoint document library holding these documents. We go into where each file is stored later in this book.

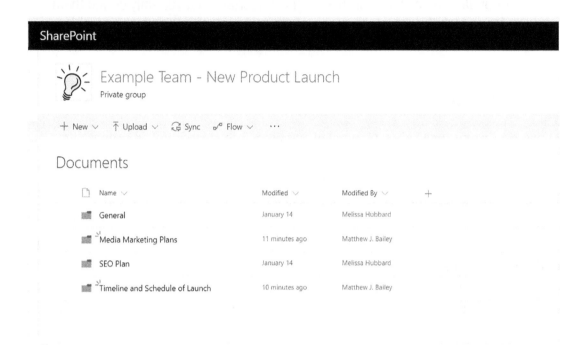

Figure 1-5. A document library created in SharePoint Online from a team

Using the SharePoint Site Collection Outside of Teams

Whether or not we should encourage people to use the SharePoint site collection for other reasons (workflows, lists, etc.) is a good question that depends on your own reasoning. At the moment, the only portion of the SharePoint site collection that automatically appears in Microsoft Teams is the Shared Documents folder. You can use other parts of SharePoint, but you have to add them as a link from a tab or by adding cloud storage.

One potential upside of using the SharePoint site collection outside of the Teams interface is that SharePoint has much greater granular security, and this is one way to overcome the current limitation of no channel-based security in Teams. The downside of this, however, is that you are opening both Microsoft Teams and SharePoint to manage different artifacts.

Caution   Although you can put other things into a SharePoint site collection to add to the channel tab for easy access, changing the channels' folder structure does **not** update the channels in Teams. It is important that you only create them from the Teams interface.

Groups and Teams

Office 365 Groups (or Modern Groups) places users into meaningful groupings that allow you to set notifications or security across many applications. Technically, an Office 365 group is an object in Azure Active Directory. It can have one or many members and be used across most Office 365 applications. For example, you may have a marketing department with salespeople working with them. You might create a group called Marketing, add all of the employees from that area to this group, and then add the group to the application(s) you are using. This is much easier to manage than repeatedly adding each user individually to each application for security and notifications.

The reason that Office 365 Groups matter in conjunction with Microsoft Teams is because an Office 365 group is the parent of a team. Whenever you create a new team, it creates an Office 365 group (unless you select to create a team from an existing Office 365 group). You also choose whether the team is private or public (the group is of this same type). But in either case, behind the scenes, there is a group at a higher level that controls your team's security and other features. The relationship between Office 365 Groups and Teams becomes far more important later in the book as we dive into Teams administration. For now, just understand that an Office 365 group is one of the many pieces working to make your team function properly.

Exchange/Outlook and Teams

Like other Office 365 applications that Microsoft Teams interacts with, Exchange only enables all of its benefits when it is fully online in the Office 365 suite. Although you can use Exchange On-Premises or Exchange dedicated (legacy) with Microsoft Teams, some functionality works and some does not. As a note, users hosted on Exchange Online or Exchange Dedicated vNext have access to all the features in Microsoft Teams.

The key takeaway is that Microsoft Teams uses Exchange to create a group mailbox that stores the team's information, such as meetings (messages are stored in a SharePoint folder). To see which functionalities are enabled or disabled (this depends on your version of Exchange), please visit the Microsoft website at `https://docs.microsoft.com/en-us/microsoftteams/exchange-teams-interact`.

Note   For the full Microsoft Teams experience, every user should be enabled for Exchange Online, SharePoint Online, and Office 365 Groups creation.

OneDrive for Business and Teams

OneDrive for Business is used a bit within Microsoft Teams. Mostly, it is where files that are shared from a team chat are stored (not a channel conversation). Permissions to the files are restricted automatically so that only the intended user can access them.

Summary

This chapter explained Microsoft Teams and the history of the platform, and reviewed its core functionality. In the next chapter, we take a look at the components and how we get work done within a team.

CHAPTER 2

Working in Teams

Teams and their channels are the heart of user collaboration and productivity. Although Microsoft Teams can be used just for chatting and holding meetings, the true power of the application is recognized by adding teams and channels and knowing how to retrieve information from them. This chapter provides information and instructions on how to maximize working with Microsoft Teams. We explore creating teams, channels, and tabs, as well as searching by using the @commands and shortcuts.

What you can and cannot do in Microsoft Teams is based on the permission role you have. There are currently three roles available in Teams:

- Team member

- Team owner

- Guest (must be enabled by your administrator)

By default, anyone within an organization can create a team. When they do, they become the team owner. In Table 2-1, you see what default actions team members and team owners have the ability to do when working in Teams. Some of these default actions can also be modified by the team owner.

Note   Guests are people that are not part of an organization and do not have an account in the organization's Active Directory.

© Melissa Hubbard, Matthew J. Bailey 2018
M. Hubbard and M. J. Bailey, *Mastering Microsoft Teams*, https://doi.org/10.1007/978-1-4842-3670-3_2

Table 2-1. *Default Owner and Team Member Settings in a New Team*

Action	Team Member	Team Owner	Guest
Creating a team		X	
Editing a team		X	
Deleting a team		X	
Adding team members		X	
Adding a channel	X	X	
Editing a channel	X	X	
Deleting a channel	X	X	
Getting channel email	X	X	X
Getting channel link	X	X	X
Favoriting a channel	X	X	X
Following a channel	X	X	X
Managing channels	X	X	
Uploading files	X	X	X
Deleting files	X	X	X
Downloading files	X	X	X
Adding tabs	X	X	
Deleting tabs	X	X	
Adding connectors	X	X	

Teams

Teams are a central location where a group of people with common work functions can hold conversations, collaborate on content, and create work products. Teams are the container for channels and tabs. The first step to setting up a team is creating the team itself; then, you can build upon the functionality by adding channels, tabs, and connectors. Let's get started!

Note   Users must be enabled for Office 365 Groups to create teams in Microsoft Teams.

Creating a Team

To create a team

1. Click **Add team**, located on the bottom left in the Teams app, as seen in Figure 2-1.

2. Click the **Create team** button.

3. Enter a team name, description, and privacy settings.

4. Add team members. A person's name, distribution list, or mail-enabled security group can be selected.

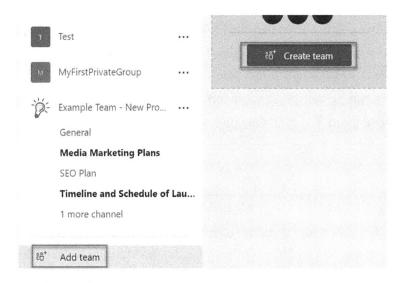

Figure 2-1. *Creating a team*

Be sure to name your team something meaningful. Although it is optional, it is recommended to enter a description for the team. As more and more teams are added, a description helps people in the organization determine which public team they should join.

You also need to decide on the privacy for the new team. If you don't change the setting, it defaults to private. This means that only team owners can add team members. There is also the option to make a team public, which means that anyone in the organization that has a Microsoft Teams license can join.

Note   It is important to make sure that a team with the name that you plan to use does not already exist. Nothing stops you from creating a name that is the same as another team; however, doing so can create confusion and other issues for your users.

Another option is to create a team from an existing Office 365 group. When creating a new team, first click the link at the bottom of the window that says Join or create a team. Next, click the *Create a team* button. A window will then appear with a link to select titled *Create a team from an existing Office 365 group*. You are given a list of groups you are the owner of to choose from. Once you select the group, you can create the team. Everyone that is part of the group is added as members of the team.

Note   Teams can be reordered in the left navigation by dragging and dropping them where you want them. The channels that are part of the team are moved with it.

Managing a Team

When you create a new team, there are only a limited number of options available to configure its settings. Much of this is done by using the **Manage team** option. Within this area of a team, you have the option to change the overall settings for everyone on the team. This includes setting the overall permissions for what internal and guest users can do. You can also determine whether @mentions and fun stuff like emojis or animated GIFs can be used, and change the team picture (icon).

CHAPTER 2   WORKING IN TEAMS

Let's review how to add a team picture.

1. Click the ellipse (...) to the right of the team name, and then select **Manage team**.

2. Select the Settings tab, and then select the team picture. Expand the section. Click the **Change picture** link and select the picture. In the pop-up box, locate the image that you want to use.

3. Click the **Save** button.

Editing a Team

Situations may arise when there is a need to change the name or description of a team, such as an organizational change, another team in your organization with the same name, or team member feedback.

To edit a team name

1. Click the ellipse (...) to the right of the team name, and then select **Edit team**, as seen in Figure 2-2.

2. Change the team name, description, and privacy settings as desired.

3. Click the **Done** button.

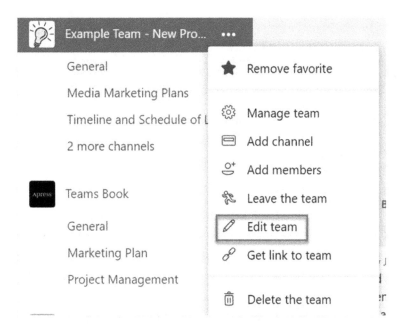

Figure 2-2. *Editing a team name, privacy setting, or description*

Adding Team Members

Team owners have the ability to add team members to both private and public teams.
To add team members

1.   Click the ellipse (…) to the right of the name, and then select
     Add members, as seen in Figure 2-3.

2.   Begin typing the name of the person, distribution list, or
     mail-enabled security group that you wish to add to the team.

3.   Click **Add**.

The people that you add will receive a notification email that they have been added
to the team.

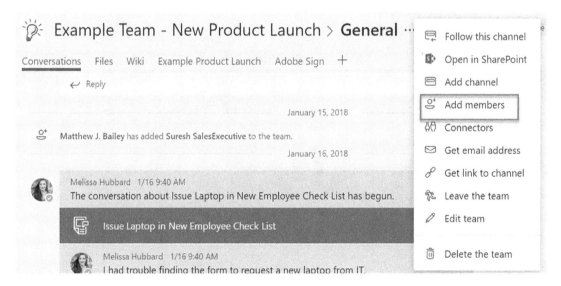

Figure 2-3. *Adding team members*

Deleting a Team

When a team is deleted, all the channels, chat, files, and the Office 365 group is
deleted. When the team is deleted, it is held in the tenant's "recycle bin" in Azure
Active Directory (AAD) for 30 days and referred to as being in a "soft-delete" status.
During this time, the team can be restored using PowerShell, which requires the
assistance of an administrator. It can take up to 24 hours for a deleted team to reappear

after being restored. After 30 days have passed without being restored, however, the team is permanently deleted in the environment and cannot be recovered by anyone, including Microsoft.

To delete a team

1. Click the ellipse (...) to the right of the team name, and then select **Delete the team**, as seen in Figure 2-4.

2. Click the box stating that you understand that everything is deleted.

3. Click the **Delete team** button.

Note In some cases, Office 365 Groups are used for purposes outside of Microsoft Teams. There is no way to delete the team and keep the group for other purposes.

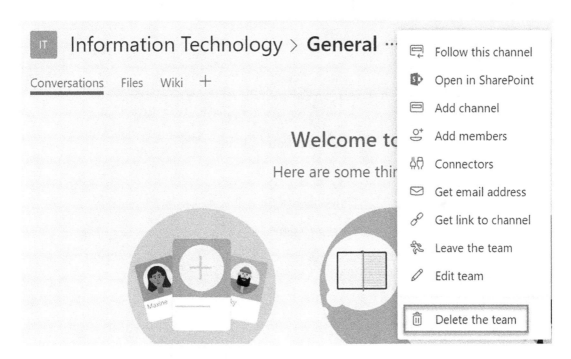

Figure 2-4. *Deleting a team*

Channels

Channels within a team provide a means to separate content and conversations for different projects, subjects, organizations, or disciplines. One organization we worked with created a separate team for every IT project. Within those teams, they created channels for different work functions on the project, such as development, quality assurance, and project management.

When viewing teams, the channels fall underneath them in the application navigation. Every person that is part of a team can access every channel, as in the example shown in Figure 2-5.

Note It is not possible to make a channel have a different membership than the team it is part of. Members of a team can view all content within every channel. Microsoft might add a feature at some point to allow securing channels to certain users; however, it was not available when writing this book.

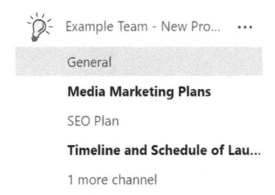

Figure 2-5. *A team with channels in the left navigation*

Adding a Channel

By default, every person that is part of a team can create a channel for that team. Whenever a team is created, it automatically comes with a General channel. This channel should be used for team conversations and content related to the overall goals and objectives. When there is a need to collaborate and discuss something more specific, it is recommended to create a new channel. Before creating a channel, it is important to make sure that there is not already a channel being used for your planned topic. In Chapter 6, we discuss appropriate reasons to create a channel.

To add a channel

1. Click the ellipse (...) to the right of the team name, and then select **Add channel**, as seen in Figure 2-6.

2. Provide a name and a description for the channel.

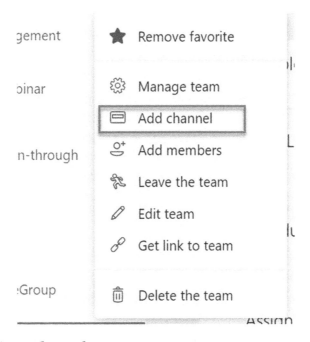

Figure 2-6. *Adding a channel*

When prompted to provide a name, be sure to name your channel something meaningful. Although it is optional, it is recommended to enter a description for the channel. As a team grows and more channels are added, descriptions help team members determine where they should have conversations and collaborate. A meaningful channel name and description can also avoid duplication of channels. If the name is unrecognizable and there is no description, another team member may create a channel that contains similar content and conversations.

Editing a Channel

As the content and conversations evolve within a channel, there may be a need to change the name or description of the channel.

To edit the channel name or description

1. Click the ellipse (...) next to the channel name, and then click **Edit this channel**.

2. Change the channel name or description.

3. Click **Save**.

Deleting a Channel

While an organization goes through the process of adopting Microsoft Teams, the need to delete a channel is bound to come up. Since any member of a team can create a channel by default, it is likely that someone will accidently create a channel or experiment with creating one without actually needing the channel. For example, a channel may be created for a topic that already has an active channel. In this case, the channel with the least amount of content should be deleted. Another circumstance that leads to deletion is when the channel limit is reached. There can only be as many as 200 channels for each team. For most teams, 200 channels should be more than enough, but if the limit is approaching, it may be necessary to delete channels that are not being used often or at all.

When a channel is deleted, all conversations and tabs are deleted along with the channel. The channel can be restored, but it cannot be re-created with the same name as a blank slate. What this means is that you can restore a channel you deleted but you cannot reuse the name of a channel you deleted again later.

To delete a channel

1. Click the ellipse (...) next to the channel name, and then click **Delete this channel**.

2. Click the **Delete** button, as seen in Figure 2-7.

When you delete a channel, you are provided a link to the folder where channel files are located. Since the files are stored in SharePoint, they are not deleted when the channel is deleted.

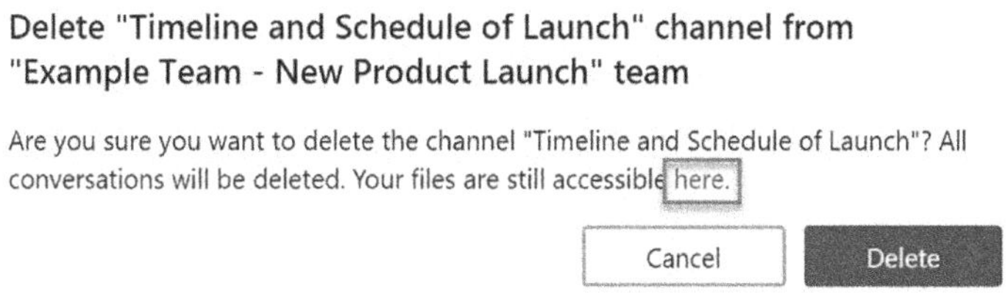

Delete "Timeline and Schedule of Launch" channel from
"Example Team - New Product Launch" team

Are you sure you want to delete the channel "Timeline and Schedule of Launch"? All
conversations will be deleted. Your files are still accessible here.

Cancel   Delete

Figure 2-7. *File link when deleting a channel*

To delete channel files

1. Navigate to the *General* channel and select the *Files* tab.

2. Click **Open in SharePoint**. This opens the team document library
   in your Internet browser showing a view of the channel folder.

3. Click **Documents** to the left of the channel name.

4. Click the check mark to the left of the channel name folder, and
   then click **Delete**.

Restoring a Channel

If a deleted channel needs to be restored, this can be done quickly with the restore
channel functionality.

To restore a channel

1. Click the ellipse (…) to the right of the team name, and then select
   Manage team.

2. Select the Channels tab. If any channels have been deleted, they
   show up in the deleted section.

3. Click **Restore**.

Channel Email

Every channel comes with an email address. When the channel is emailed, it creates a
new conversation thread in Teams. The email address of the person that emailed the
channel is shown at the top of the conversation. The subject of the email appears in
bold letters; this is followed by the email body. There is also a link to the original email,

which is accessible to anyone in the organization but not external guests. When that link is clicked, it opens the email in Outlook. If the user is not logged in to Outlook, they are prompted to do so. All email messages are saved in a subfolder called Emails in the channel folder.

This channel email functionality is meant to deter important messages from being lost in endless email threads. Often, people miss information when someone forgets to Reply All when responding to an email, or forwards it to someone else. The channel email helps avoid these blunders. Additionally, when new team members come aboard, it is much easier to get them up to speed when they can read through conversations in a channel.

To get the channel email address

1. Click the ellipse (...) to the right of the channel name, and then click **Get email address**.

2. Click the **Copy** button, as seen in Figure 2-8.

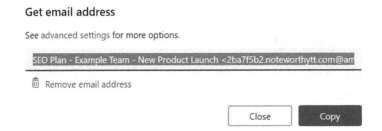

Get email address

See advanced settings for more options.

SEO Plan - Example Team - New Product Launch <2ba7f5b2.noteworthytt.com@am

🗑 Remove email address

Close   Copy

Figure 2-8.   *Channel email address*

The email address is displayed along with links to advanced settings and to remove the email address. The email address is generated by the system and cannot be changed. The Copy button can quickly capture the email address to paste into an email.

You can control who can send an email to the channel email address by clicking the advanced settings link. By default, anyone—even people who are not a member of the team or the organization—can send an email to a channel email address. You can choose to have only team members able to email the channel email address, or to have emails only sent from certain domains. Examples of email domains are @hotmail.com, @gmail.com, @noteworthytt.com, and @melihubb.com.

If the **Remove email address** button is clicked, the email address is disabled. If anyone tries to email the channel once an email address is removed, they will receive a delivery failure.

Note   If the channel email address is removed, it cannot be recovered. Only remove the email if you are absolutely sure you do not want the channel email address functionality.

Channel Link

In some instances, you may want to refer a channel to someone that hasn't yet adopted Microsoft Teams and doesn't know what a channel is or how to find one. Also, members of an organization may be part of several teams, and each team may have many channels. In this case, you can simply provide a team member a link to the channel, and they can paste it into an Internet browser. They are then prompted to open the channel in the Teams app, if they have it installed, or they can view the channel within the browser. If someone who is not a member of the team tries to use the link, they will not be able to access the channel.

To get the channel link

1. Click the ellipse (…) to the right of the channel name, and then click **Get a link to the channel**.

2. Click the **Copy** button, as seen in Figure 2-9.

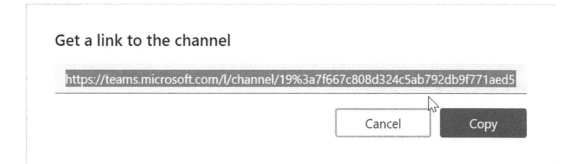

Figure 2-9. Channel link

Favoriting a Channel

To keep up with the conversations and content in a channel, team members have the ability to favorite and follow channels. When a channel is favorited, the member sees the channel name in the list under the team name. If a channel is not favorited, the member needs to click more channels underneath the last favorited channel in the list to view it. When a channel is @mentioned in a conversation, all members that have it favorited receive a notification. @mentions is discussed in Chapter 3. By default, when a member is added to a team, the five most active channels are automatically favorited. If there are fewer than five channels, any new channels are automatically added as favorites when they are created, until there are five.

To favorite a channel

1. Click the arrow next to **more channels** underneath the team name, as seen in Figure 2-10.

2. Click the star to the right of the channel name.

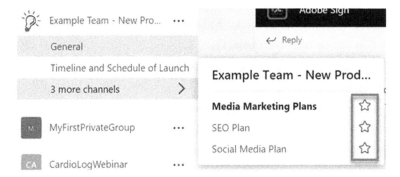

Figure 2-10. *Favoriting a channel*

Following a Channel

When a channel is followed, the member receives a notification whenever a new conversation message is added. There is also an activity feed in which members can view all recent conversations in the channels they are following. It is recommended that a member only follow the channels that have the most importance to them. Depending on how active a channel is, a lot of notifications may be sent out. If a member follows too many channels, they may begin to ignore the notifications all together, which render them useless.

To follow a channel

1. Click the ellipse (…) next to the channel name, and then click **Follow this channel**, as seen in Figure 2-11.

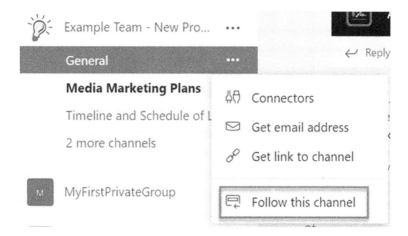

Figure 2-11. *Following a channel*

Note   The activity feed shows team members all activity of channels they follow as well as mentions of them or any team or channel they are part of. It shows them replies to their conversation messages and likes of the message. All saved conversation messages are also shown. More about mentions and liking messages can be found in Chapter 3.

Managing Channels

There is a way to view and manage all channels for a team in one view. You can see the channel names and descriptions along with the number of people that follow the channel as seen in Figure 2-12. You can also see the date that the channel had its last activity. If the last activity occurred on the current day, you can see how many hours ago the activity was.

To manage channels

1. Click the ellipse (…) next to the team name, and then click **Manage team**.

2. Click **Channels**.

Members Channels Settings Bots				
Search for channels 🔍			Add channel	

Name ▲	Description	People	Last activity	
General		👥 6	1/16	•••
★ Media Marketing Pla...		👥 2	1/13	•••
★ SEO Plan		👥 6	1/20	•••
☆ Social Media Plan		👥 5	1/13	•••
★ Timeline and Schedu...		👥 2	1/13	•••

Figure 2-12. *Managing channels*

Tabs

Tabs make the customizable workspace within Microsoft Teams possible. Tabs are containers within a team's channels that hold content connected to a cloud-based service, such as what's seen in Figure 2-13. Files, websites, SharePoint lists and libraries, Planner tasks, Power BI reports, and even third-party cloud-based tools can be viewed and worked on in tabs. Every channel has its own set of tabs that can be configured. There are three tabs that come automatically with every channel: Conversations, Files, and Wiki. The Wiki tab can be deleted, but the Conversations and Files tabs cannot be deleted because they are part of core Microsoft Teams functionality.

Figure 2-13. *Tabs*

Note   If you want to focus on working in just one tab, you can expand and view it without the teams and channels list on the left part of the app or the tabs and team name at the top of the app.

Conversations Tab

Every channel within a team has a separate Conversations tab. The conversations that occur in the channels cannot be viewed together. In other words, you cannot view all team conversations from every channel in one view. Figure 2-14 provides an example. Conversations are discussed further in Chapter 3.

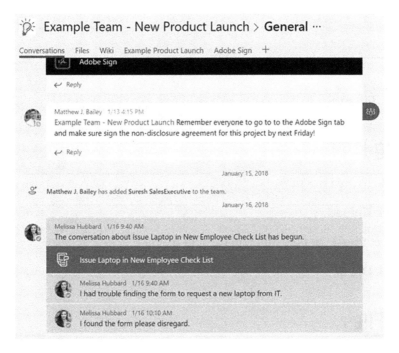

Figure 2-14. *Conversations tab*

Files Tab

The Files tab is where documents and other files are uploaded for team members to collaborate and share. An example of this is shown in Figure 2-15.

Files should only be added if they pertain to the channel topic. The Files tab should not be used as a place to store personal files. It is different from the Conversations tab in that all the files that are uploaded in the separate channel tabs live in one SharePoint document library for the team. Every channel gets a folder in the document library. When you click the Files tab in a channel, you get a view of the files in the Channel folder. The fields displayed are File type, Name, Modified, and Modified by. The modified field shows the date that the file was last changed. If this is within the current day, it shows the number of hours ago that the file was changed. The **Modified by** field shows which team member last changed the file.

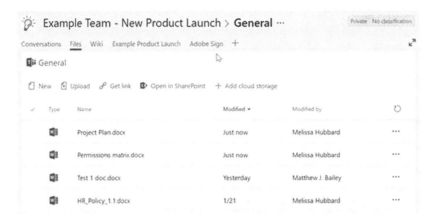

Figure 2-15. *Files tab*

Uploading Files

To upload a file to the Files tab

1. Click **Upload**.

2. Select the file or files that you want to upload.

3. Click **Open**.

Deleting Files

To delete a file from the Files tab

1. Click the document, which highlights it in blue.

2. Click **Delete**.

3. Click **Confirm**.

Note   When a file is removed from the Files tab, it is moved to the SharePoint recycle bin.

Downloading Files

To download a file from the Files tab

1. Click the document, which highlights it in blue.

2. Click **Download**. The downloaded files folder opens.

3. Select the file, and then click **Open**.

Wiki Tab

The Wiki tab as seen in Figure 2-16 quickly captures ideas and information on one central page per channel. The Wiki tab is comprised of pages and sections. When you add pages, they are displayed in a navigation pane on the left. When sections are added to a page, they appear in the navigation underneath the page that they are a part of, thus creating a table of contents–like functionality.

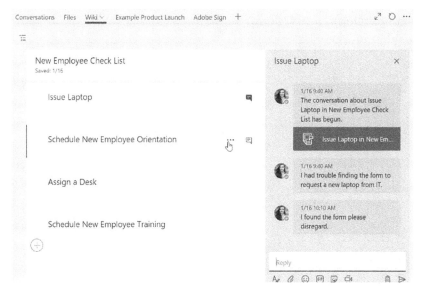

Figure 2-16. *The Wiki tab in a team displaying a conversation*

Organizations can use the wiki page to present information, such as a checklist or the steps of a process. If you create a section for each checklist item, team members can use the built-in conversations functionality to discuss the process and provide feedback. For example, if you create a wiki page for a checklist of things that need to happen when a new employee joins a project, new team members can add comments and make suggestions. All of this happens within the wiki page. The conversations appear within the wiki page, but they are also added under a channel's Conversations tab for visibility. A conversation message includes a link that brings team members to the wiki page. If someone responds to a conversation in the Conversations tab, it is also displayed in the conversation in the wiki section associated with it. There is also the ability to add additional wiki tabs to a channel.

On the back end, the wiki content is stored in the same SharePoint site collection that is created when you create a team. First, all the wiki content for that channel is placed in a document library titled Teams Wiki Data (see Figure 2-17). This folder is automatically created by the system when you create your first wiki page.

	Name	Type	Items	Modified
	Documents	Document library	1	1/24/2018 4:58 PM
	Form Templates	Document library	0	1/15/2018 8:32 PM
	Site Assets	Document library	1	1/24/2018 4:59 PM
	Style Library	Document library		
	Teams Wiki Data	Document library		
	Site Pages	Page library		

All the wiki pages are stored within the document library "Teams Wiki Data" with separate sub-folders beneath this.

Figure 2-17. *The Teams Wiki Data document library within your SharePoint site collection*

Within the Teams Wiki Data folder, there is another subfolder for each channel. Inside of each of these subfolders are the system files for each wiki. Each wiki page is stored as a .mht file, making it best to only edit wikis within Microsoft Teams and not via the SharePoint document library.

Adding a Tab

To create a tab

1. Click the plus sign that is located to the far right of the tabs area of the channel.

2. Select the connector for the service that you want to connect to and use in the tab, as seen in Figure 2-18.

The connector that you select determines the next step in adding the tab. Depending on what you select, you are prompted to select a file or a work product, or to create a new one.

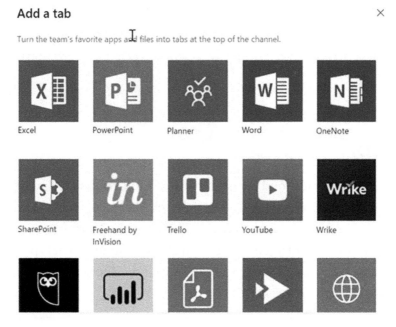

Figure 2-18. *Adding a tab*

Note   For information to be secure when adding a website to a tab, the URL needs to start with https.

Deleting a Tab

To delete a tab

1. Click the name of the tab that you want to delete.

2. Click the drop-down arrow, and then select **Remove**, as seen in Figure 2-19.

3. Click **Remove** when prompted.

The tab is deleted, but that does not mean that the file or work product displayed is deleted from the source.

Figure 2-19. *Removing a tab*

Connectors

Connectors are a gateway to cloud services that Microsoft Teams can interact with. The connectors are contained within tabs in the channel. Microsoft Teams connects with many Office 365 apps, such as Planner, Excel, and OneNote. Third-party services—such as Trello, Twitter, GitHub, and Smartsheet—can also be connected. It is possible to create custom connectors using a web hook. You can learn more about developing custom connectors from Microsoft's website.

Note   If the team member who created a connector is removed from the team, the connector stops working until another teammate re-creates it.

To add a connector

1. Click the ellipse (…) next to the channel name, and then click **Connectors**.

2. Search for the service of choice, and then click the **Configure** button, as seen in Figure 2-20.

3. Log in to the service.

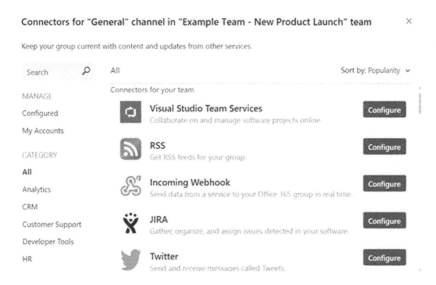

Figure 2-20. Adding a connector

It is important to remember that a connector is a connection to another service that can read and write data to and from your organization. In a way, this a great benefit: you do not have to leave the Microsoft Teams client. Your administrators might find it to be a data or security risk, however. In the Office 365 administration center, you can disable or enable each connector separately so that only the options vetted for your organization can be used.

Search

Searching in Microsoft Teams is a bit basic, although there are some filtering options available. If you are used to a rich, sortable, minutely refined search experience such as what exists in SharePoint, unfortunately, you will not find that in Microsoft Teams yet. You need to search to find the files that you work with, so let's review the options that are available and go over how to use them to best extent possible.

The search experience begins with a combined search and command bar, as seen in Figure 2-21. It is rather self-explanatory: you just type what you are searching for. This performs a broad search across all of your teams. The results are returned within one or more of the following filtering categories:

- Messages

- People

- Files

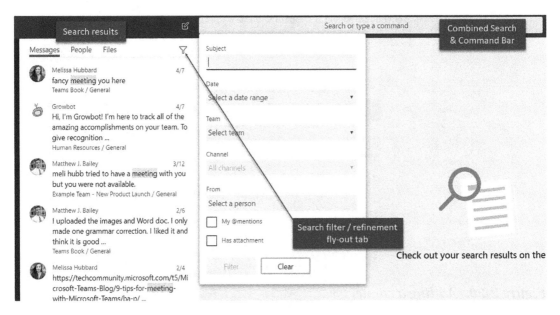

Figure 2-21. *The search experience in Microsoft Teams*

The Messages category returns results from your private chats, channel conversations that are posted for all to see within a team channel, conversations you have with bots, and emails sent to a team.

It does not return the results from the wiki, meeting titles, or documents in your Files tab, such as OneDrive for Business, Dropbox, or Google Drive.

The People category is used to find persons within your organization. If you want to find data from a specific person, you want to use the Filter tab.

The Files tab returns Word, Excel, PowerPoint, and OneNote files, images, text files, and PDFs. Teams returns the results of the search term, which appears within the filename or within the body of text. It also searches within .zip files for contents containing your search phrase.

Note   Content Search allows you to search across most of the components of Teams, including Exchange, SharePoint, and OneDrive for Business. It is only available to administrators using the Office 365 administration center.

Using the Search Filter

As teams and the amount of content grows larger, attempting to find content can be difficult. To refine the search results, you can utilize the Filter tab (pane). The Filter tab only appears in Messages and Files (there is no filter option for the People category). As you can see in Figure 2-22, you can refine by team, file type, and/or the person who last worked on the file.

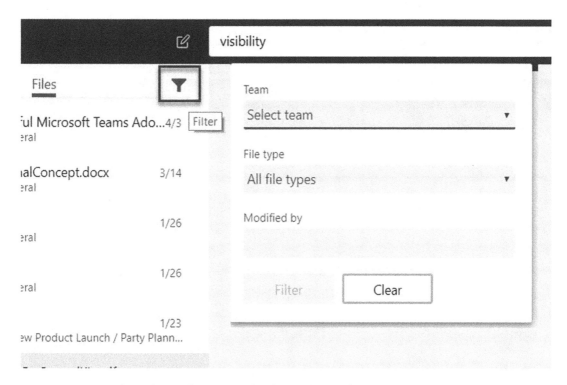

Figure 2-22. *The Filter tab in search alters, depending on which category you have highlighted*

Quick Commands and the Command Bar

The command bar is combined with the search box. Quick commands are shortcuts that perform an action or return some type of data. Quick commands start with / or @ symbols.

@commands

@commands are a way to search within a specific context. If you are familiar with searching in Google for a word within the title of a web result by using Title:MyWord, the @command exemplifies a similar feature except within the context of a user (like @mentioning someone on Twitter) or within the context of an installed app. By typing the @ symbol, you receive a list of users and apps that you can use the @command with. In Figure 2-23, we used the @Weather command.

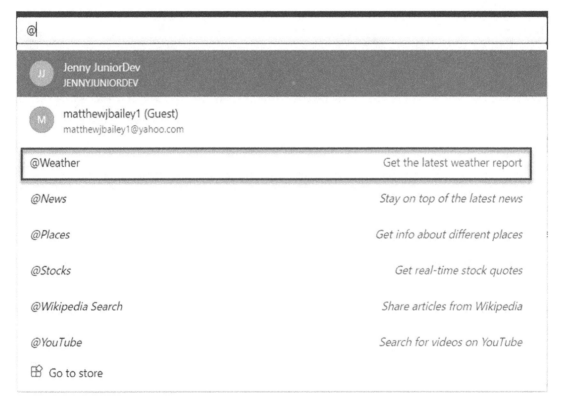

Figure 2-23. *Using the @Weather command in the command bar*

After selecting the @Weather command, the command bar then prefaces any search you perform with the Weather app. You are now able to search for the weather in cities across the world (see Figure 2-24).

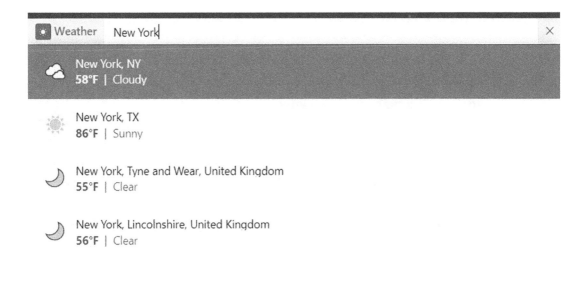

Figure 2-24. *Selecting a city to use with the @Weather command to return the current weather for that city*

Note   If you use an @command for an app that you do not have installed, you are prompted to install the app.

/commands

Slash commands (/commands), or shortcuts, in the command bar provide another way to quickly perform a task or obtain data. At the time we write this book, there are less than 20 slash commands available to users. It is highly likely that this number will increase as Microsoft Teams grows in popularity. The following is a list of available slash commands:

- /activity: View a team member's activity

- /available: Changes your team's status to Available

- /away: Changes your team's status to Away

- /busy: Changes your team's status to Busy

- /call: Initiate a call
- /dnd: Changes your team's status to Do Not Disturb
- /files: See your recent files
- /goto: Go to a certain team or channel
- /help: Get help (with Teams; not the "lie on the couch" kind)
- /join: Join a team
- /keys: View keyboard shortcuts
- /mentions: See all of your mentions (Handy if your team's channels are really busy!)
- /org: View an org chart (yours or someone else's)
- /saved: View your saved list
- /unread: See all of your unread activity
- /whatsnew: Check out what's new in Teams
- /who: Ask Who (a new app that lets you search for people by name or topic) a question

The following covers some of the more popular slash commands.

/activity

/activity helps you find data when you can't remember exactly what a file is called, but you do remember who worked on it last. It can also come in handy if someone left your project, and you want to see what they were working on recently so that you can reassign it to someone else.

/dnd, /busy, /away, /available

/dnd, /busy, /away, and /available offer quick and easy ways to change your notification status. Although it may take a couple of seconds, these commands change the colored icon next to your name to alert others of your availability. The /dnd command sets your status to Do Not Disturb and automatically forwards calls to your voice mail. The other three slash commands provide a visual indicator that indicates whether you are available or not. These commands do not prevent someone from calling or messaging you the way that the /dnd command does.

/who

The /who command triggers the Who Bot, which is used to find specific people (and more detailed information about them) within your organization. If you have not used it before, it prompts you to allow it to perform searches on your behalf. An example of this experience is seen in Figure 2-25.

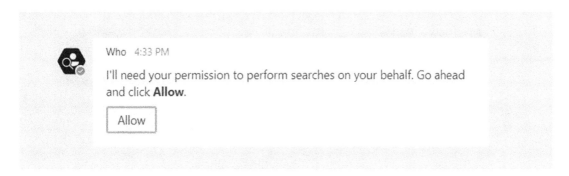

Figure 2-25. *The Who Bot asking for permission to search on your behalf*

If for some reason more than one result returns, you are prompted to select the result that you are searching for (see Figure 2-26).

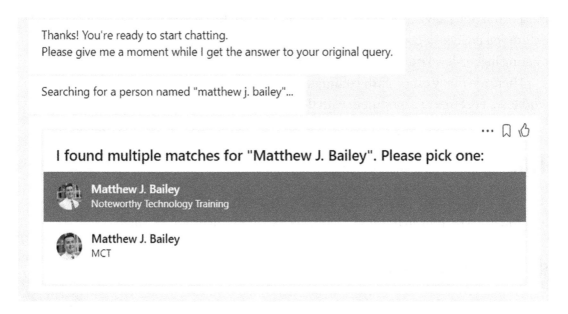

Figure 2-26. *Displays the results from the Who Bot if you receive more than one result*

After selecting the correct person that you want to inquire about, a *card* displays more information about the user, as seen in Figure 2-27.

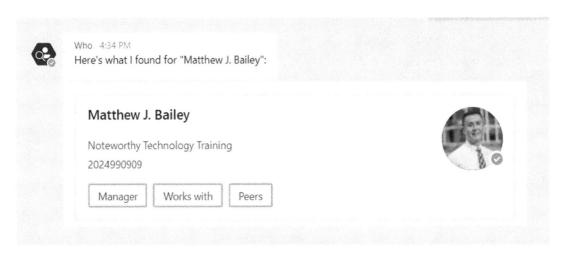

Figure 2-27. *A card with information about the person you are searching for*

From here, you can find activity-based information, such as who the person works with, their manager, and their peers. This can be helpful if the person is out on leave, for example, and you need to find someone who is able to assist you with the responsibilities this person normally has. It can also be used to learn the person's level of management before you engage in conversation with them, since there is usually an expectation of treating higher-level executives in a formal manner.

There are many other slash commands available in Teams to accelerate your workload. Feel free to experiment with them yourself.

Tips

As we wrap up this chapter on how to work efficiently in Microsoft Teams, let's discuss a few quick tips on how to improve your working experience even further.

Keyboard Shortcuts

First, let's discuss keyboard shortcuts. You can see all of the available shortcuts by pressing **ALT**+/ on your keyboard. After doing so, you should see something similar to what's shown in Figure 2-28.

Keyboard shortcuts   ✕

General

Show keyboard shortcuts	Alt /	Go to Search		Alt E
List commands	Alt K	Jump to goto command	Alt Shift	G
Start new chat	Alt N	Open Settings		Alt G
Open Help	Alt H	Close		Esc
Zoom in	Ctrl =	Zoom out		Ctrl -

Navigation

Open Activity	Alt 1	Open Chat		Alt 2
Open Teams	Alt 3	Open Meetings		Alt 4
Open Files	Alt 5	Go to previous list item		Alt ↑
Go to next list item	Alt ↓	Go to previous tab		Alt ←
Go to next tab	Alt →	Move selected team up	Ctrl Shift	↑
Move selected team down	Ctrl Shift ↓			

Messaging

Focus compose box	C	Expand compose box		Alt X
Send (expanded compose box)	Ctrl Enter	Attach file		Alt A
Start new line	Shift Enter	Reply to thread		R

Meetings and Calls

Accept video call	Ctrl Shift A	Accept audio call	Ctrl Shift	S
Decline call	Ctrl Shift D	Start audio call	Ctrl Shift	C
Start video call	Ctrl Shift U	Toggle mute	Ctrl Shift	M
Toggle video	Ctrl Shift O	Toggle fullscreen	Ctrl Shift	F
Go to sharing toolbar	Ctrl Shift Space			

See shortcuts for all platforms   Office Accessibility Center

Figure 2-28. *A listing of the shortcut keys available in Microsoft Teams*

Some of these keyboard shortcuts are available in Windows and some of them are specific to Teams and Skype for Business. Feel free to experiment with them to see which ones work best for you.

Ctrl+K (Adding a Link)

Although there are keys to add attachments, animated GIFs, start a meeting, and change the fonts in a conversation, there isn't a button to add a hyperlink. By pressing Ctrl+K on the keyboard, you can quickly add a link to the text you are typing. As seen in Figure 2-29, you can type the display text and the URL that the link goes to. We use this often by creating statements such as, "Please find the document to review **here**."

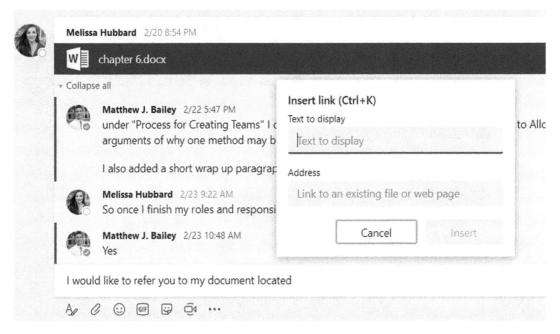

Figure 2-29. *Adding a link to a channel conversation by selecting Ctrl+K*

Summary

We have now reviewed the components inside a team that enable you to complete your work. We have explored channels, tabs, and connectors. We investigated different ways to retrieve data with search, @commands, and keyboard shortcuts. Now let's continue our journey by learning about the different ways to communicate within Teams.

CHAPTER 3

Communicating in Teams

Microsoft Teams offers a suite of communication tools that empower team members to be engaged and collaborative with one another. In the modern world, team members are on the go and often work from remote locations away from their team. Having reliable virtual communication options is absolutely essential to drive productivity by working together and making decisions. In this chapter, we'll discuss voice, video, imagery, chat, and other ways to communicate in Microsoft Teams.

Conversations

Conversations occur within team channels. They provide a place where team members can discuss topics and post messages in which everyone in the team can reply.

One of the biggest benefits of conversations is a reduction in email. Conversations differ from traditional email in that they are all in one viewable area for all team members. Email messages are stored within individual mail inboxes, which limits visibility for team members. Oftentimes, someone sends out an email about a topic to a group of people. Then, that email is replied to without including the entire group, or forwarded to an individual and the group context is lost. This results in team members being excluded from the series of emails and being left in the dark about key decisions and discussions related to the topic.

One of the key values in using conversations is that it preserves your organizational assets. In conversations, important information can be passed and decisions made between team members. If all the team members leave the organization, the information remains in the channel for you and others to view at a later time. When a new member joins the organization, department, or project, they are able to get up to speed. Having conversations stored in Microsoft Teams allows them to go to one place to read through conversations and quickly get up to speed.

© Melissa Hubbard, Matthew J. Bailey 2018

M. Hubbard and M. J. Bailey, *Mastering Microsoft Teams*, https://doi.org/10.1007/978-1-4842-3670-3_3

To start a conversation

1. Navigate to the Conversations tab of the channel of choice.

2. At the bottom of the Conversations tab, use the text box to type your message, and then click the arrow located on the bottom-right of the text box.

Note   It is possible to create conversation messages in some of the tabs. Click the tab name, and then the chat symbol on the right, as seen in Figure 3-1.

Figure 3-1. *Beginning a conversation within a tab*

Mentioning a Team Member, Channel, or Team

If you type the @ symbol followed by a team member's name, a channel name, or a team name, a list of names that start with the few letters you type will show up for you to choose from. If you choose a person, they will receive a notification of the mention. If you choose a channel, everyone who favorited the channel receives a notification. If you choose a team, everyone who is part of the team receives a notification. This is a way to let a team member, channel, or team know that a message is directed to them and that they need to pay attention.

Liking a Message

One way to acknowledge that you have read someone's conversation message or that you agree with them is to hit the Like button on their message. This is similar to Facebook's well-known Like functionality. The person who originally posted the conversation message is notified that you liked it. You can unlike a conversation by clicking the same button.

To like messages

1. Hover your mouse over the right corner of the message.

2. Click the thumbs-up icon, which turns it blue (see Figure 3-2).

Figure 3-2. *Liking a message*

Saving a Conversation Message

Conversation messages can be saved by hitting the Save button on a message. They can be viewed later in a central location.

To save messages

1. Hover your mouse over the right corner of the message.

2. Click the **Save** icon, which turns it pink (see Figure 3-3).

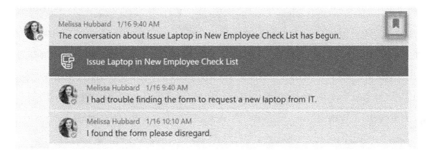

Figure 3-3. *Saving a message*

To view saved messages

1. Click your picture icon in the bottom-left corner of the Microsoft Teams app.

2. Click **Saved**, as seen in Figure 3-4.

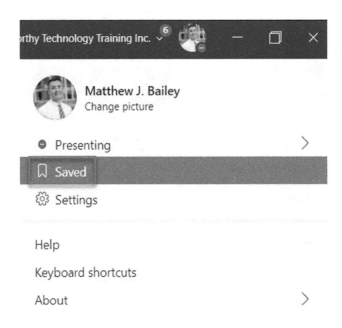

Figure 3-4. *Viewing all saved messages*

Chat

Chat in Microsoft Teams provides a way to have a 1:1 or ad hoc group conversation that provides immediate notification. If you utilized Skype for Business, you've experienced chat capability. Chat provides immediate notification. It differs from conversations in that if a team member is not following that channel, they will not be notified. Microsoft Teams also offers group chat capability. When choosing who to send a chat message to, you can choose individuals or groups.

In today's modern work centers, information workers often don't pay attention to phone calls and other forms of distraction due to loss of productivity. With the mobile app, chat can be used as a replacement for text messaging in scenarios where you may not have a co-worker's direct phone number. Team members can send a chat message and the recipient will receive it within the mobile application. Chat improves real-time communication by increasing productivity through enabling team members to hold quick discussions and get answers to questions no matter if they are in the office or on the go. Group chat improves productivity for teams by reducing meetings and meeting times through allowing teams to quickly reach decision points and discuss issues and tasks related to projects in real-time communication.

To send a chat message

1. Click the chat icon located on the left in the Teams app.

2. Click the new chat paper-and-pencil icon to the right of the Search box.

3. Enter the name(s) or group that you want to message.

4. Type your message in the text box, and then click the arrow at the bottom right of the text box.

Everyone you sent the message to will receive a notification

Chat Message Formatting Options

Expanding the compose box shows more options for the chat text. To expand the compose box, click the symbol with the letter A and a paint brush below the text box, as seen in Figure 3-5.

When you do this, the functions to change the text font, size, and color will appear, as well as paragraph-formatting options, such as headings and bullets. The function to add a hyperlink is also found when you expand the compose box.

Figure 3-5. *Additional message formatting options*

Note   To mark a chat message as important, click the exclamation mark (!) symbol in the expanded compose box. The team member that you send it to will receive an email letting them know that they have received an important message.

Using Emojis

Emojis allow team members to express emotions in chats and conversations. Emojis deliver the Web 2.0 functionality that is found on popular social media platforms. They enable organizations with a tool to inject personality into projects and express more context. They feature various faces to let your teammates know how you feel about a topic or message. If you are the manager of a project and reach a project milestone that you are excited about, you can express this to your team members with an excited emoji. If you miss a deadline, you can communicate this with a sad or embarrassed emoji. In work-related scenarios such as a promotion party for a team member or planning a happy hour event, emojis enable personality-based communication to add additional feeling to a project or task being managed in Microsoft Teams. If you don't know what a particular emoji means, you can place your cursor over the emoji to see its meaning, or you can use the search box. Emojis really let a person's personality be reflected within their words.

To add an emoji to a chat or conversation message

1.   Click the smiley face icon below the text box when adding a new chat or conversation message.

2.   Either scroll through the emoji faces or use the search box to find an emotion, as seen in Figure 3-6.

Figure 3-6. *Adding emojis to a message*

Stickers

Stickers are editable images that can be sent in chat and conversation messages. Microsoft Teams comes with a wide variety of sticker templates. Stickers are a great way to have fun with your team. Teams comes with images that you can edit with text to express emotions with a picture and customized message.

To add a sticker to a chat or conversation message

1. Click the square smiley sticker icon below the text box when adding a new chat or conversation message, as seen in Figure 3-7.

2. Either scroll through the stickers or use the search box.

3. Enter any desired text, and then click the **Done** button.

49

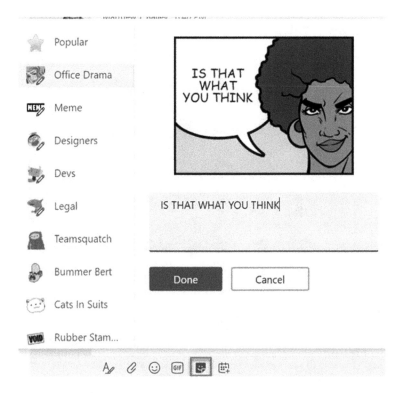

Figure 3-7. *Adding stickers to a message*

GIFs

GIF, which stands for Graphics Interchange Format, is a type of file format that supports animated images. GIFs are similar to stickers but the animation adds extra excitement and effect. You cannot add words to GIFs like you can with stickers, though. Microsoft Teams comes with many GIFs that can be used in chat and conversation messages.

To add a GIF to a chat or conversation message

1. Click the GIF icon below the text box when adding a new chat or conversation message.

2. Either scroll through the GIFs or use the search box, as seen in Figure 3-8.

3. Click the GIF of choice.

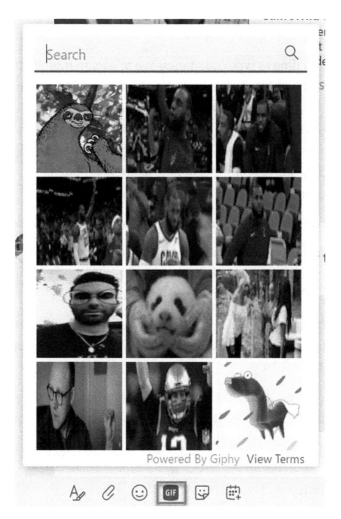

Figure 3-8. *Adding GIFs to a message*

Searching for a Message

You can search for old messages from your chat list or channel conversations. Use the search bar to enter the person's name that messaged you, or use key words from the message. You can filter your search results based on the subject, author, and date of the message.

Voice Calls

Sometimes there is no time to type a chat message to a team member, or the context of the communication requires speaking. Voice calls are perfect for this situation. If you have ever used Skype for Business in the workplace, you will find the functionality very similar. You can voice call anyone within your organization, even if they are not a member of any of your teams. If your organization has an Enterprise Voice license, you have the ability to call external phone numbers as well.

To make a voice call

1. Click the chat icon located on the left in the Microsoft Teams app.

2. Either select the person you want to call from your recent list or use the search box to find them. You can create a new chat to make the call by following the previous instructions.

3. Click the phone icon located on the top right of the chat message, as seen in Figure 3-9. You will then be brought to the call screen as seen in Figure 3-10.

4. The person is notified with a ringing that they are receiving a Teams call. If they answer, the call begins; if not, they are notified that they have a missed call.

Figure 3-9. *Making a voice call*

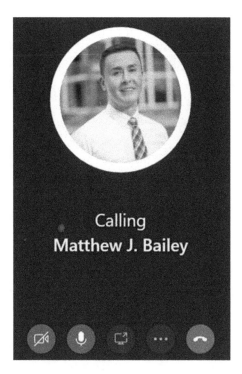

Figure 3-10. *Calling a team member*

Video Calls

Video calling is the most personal method of communication within Teams because you can both see and hear the person. With Teams video calls, the face of each person fills the entire screen, making it feel as if you are having a face-to-face conversation. You can also send chat messages while video calling a team member in case you are having trouble hearing them or want to send a link to a work product.

To make a video call

1. Click the chat icon located on the left in the Teams app.

2. Either select the person you want to video call with from your recent list or use the search box to find them. You can create a new chat to make the video call by following the previous instructions.

3. Click the video camera icon located on the top right of the chat message, as seen in Figure 3-11.

4. The person is notified with a ringing that they are receiving a Teams video call, as seen in Figure 3-12. If they answer, the call begins; if not, they are notified that they have a missed call.

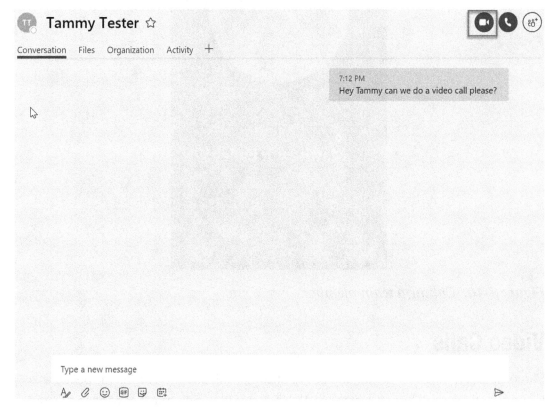

Figure 3-11. *Making a video call*

Figure 3-12. *Video calling a team member*

Choosing the Right Form of Communication

Microsoft Teams is a virtual workplace that addresses many forms of office communication. You can have one-on-one communication with a team member by using chat. The topics discussed via chat are similar to discussions one would have when stopping by a team member's office or running into them in the break area. They are informal and usually have quick response times. You can see when your team members are available, away, or offline based on the color circle on the bottom right of their profile picture. Green means available, yellow is away, red means busy, and no color means they are offline.

Group chat is similar; it is for ad hoc discussions with a group of teammates. Group chat is one way to effectively reduce the need for formal meetings, which can be a waste of time. With group chats, you can convey a message quickly to multiple team members. You can also utilize audio and video calling to see and hear your teammates, which makes it more personal. If you want to post a message that all team members can reply to on their own schedule, you should utilize conversations.

Summary

In this chapter, we explored the many options in which you can communicate with other Microsoft Teams users. We discussed how to create conversations, start voice and video calls, add emojis and images, and how to chat. Choosing the right form of communication in Microsoft Teams is important to make sure that you're conveying your messages and ideas in the best manner. Now, let's move on to the different methods of meeting with others using Microsoft Teams.

CHAPTER 4

Meetings in Teams

There has been a lot of discussion and research in the business world over the last several years about the time, money, and resources wasted on meetings. Group chat and conversations in Microsoft Teams offer practical ways to discuss topics and make decisions without taking an hour or more out of several team members' day to be in a meeting together. There are situations, however, in which meetings are necessary. Whether you are meeting to discuss status updates, do a project code review, refine a sales plan, or for any other business reason, Microsoft Teams has a way to bring you together.

There are three different meeting experiences within Microsoft Teams: private, channel, and meet now. Not only does Microsoft Teams offer different meeting experiences, there are a few different ways to both schedule and join meetings. A plethora of meeting features allow for a smooth and customizable experience. Video, voice chat, screen sharing, and chat within the meeting offer a wide range of choices for communication style. In this chapter, we discuss the meeting options in Microsoft Teams as well as how to schedule, join, and participate in them.

Private Meetings

The first type of meeting that we discuss is the most traditional in that it resembles an Outlook meeting, which is widely used. Private meetings can only be attended by team members that have been invited. They can be between two individuals, or many people. Meetings can be scheduled directly through the Microsoft Teams app or through Outlook using an add-in. If you have Microsoft Teams and either Office 2013 or Office 2016 installed on your device, the add-in shows up in Outlook automatically.

© Melissa Hubbard, Matthew J. Bailey 2018
M. Hubbard and M. J. Bailey, *Mastering Microsoft Teams*, https://doi.org/10.1007/978-1-4842-3670-3_4

Scheduling Private Meetings

To schedule a meeting through the Microsoft Teams app

1. Click the meetings icon located on the left in the Microsoft Teams app, as seen in Figure 4-1.

2. Click the **Schedule a meeting** button.

3. Fill out the title, start date and time, and end date and time, at a minimum.

4. In the **Invite people** field, select at least one person. Begin typing their name in the field, and then select them from the drop-down menu.

5. Click the **Schedule a meeting** button.

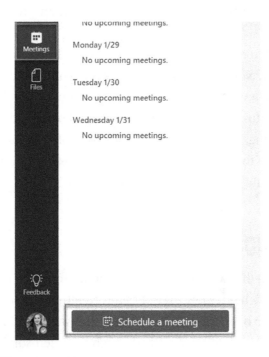

Figure 4-1. *Scheduling a meeting*

To schedule a meeting through the Outlook add-in

1. In the Outlook calendar, click the **New Teams Meeting** icon from the top ribbon, as seen in Figure 4-2.

2. Enter the meeting subject, start time, and end time.

3. Click the **Send** button.

Everyone invited will receive an email containing a link to join the meeting in Teams.

When using the Outlook add-in to schedule a Microsoft Teams meeting, you can also click New Meeting, and then select Teams Meeting. This is just a different path to get to the same destination in scheduling your meeting.

Figure 4-2. *Scheduling a meeting using the Outlook add-in*

Using the Scheduling Assistant

When scheduling a meeting, the scheduling assistant (see Figure 4-3) lets you see when attendees are busy or free during the proposed meeting time.

To use the scheduling assistant

1. Click the **Scheduling assistant** link below the end time field.

2. Decide when to hold the meeting based on the attendee's availability.

3. Click **Schedule Meeting** or **Update**, depending on if you are creating a new meeting or updating an existing one.

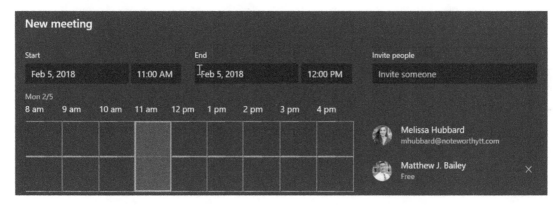

Figure 4-3.   *Using the scheduling assistant*

Inviting Unauthenticated Guests to Meetings

Teams provides a means to schedule a private meeting and invite someone that is completely outside of your organization and may not even have the Microsoft Teams app installed on their device (see Figure 4-4). The person just needs a valid email address to be invited to the private Microsoft Teams meeting and receive information on the meeting and how to join it. The guest is prompted to enter their name when they click the link to join the meeting (although guests can also join anonymously). Guests that do not have the Microsoft Teams app are not able to share their screen.

Holding virtual meetings with people from outside an organization is common. This meeting feature is useful when you need to have meetings with a client, stakeholder, contractor, vendor, or anyone that does not have an Office 365 account with your organization.

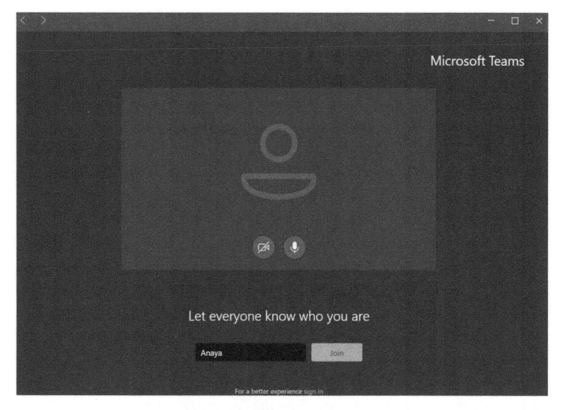

Figure 4-4. *Unauthenticated guest joining a meeting*

Joining Private Meetings

To join a meeting through the Teams app

1. Click the meetings icon located to the left of the Teams app, as seen in Figure 4-5. Any upcoming meetings you are scheduled for are shown in the Agenda section

2. Click the meeting that you wish to join, and then either click the **Join** button to the right of the meeting name or the **Join Microsoft Teams Meeting** link located in the meeting invite.

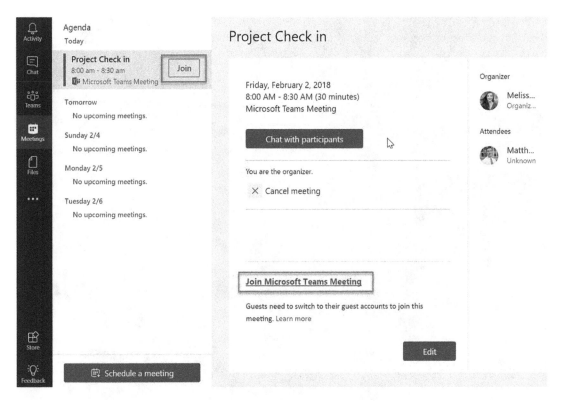

Figure 4-5. *Joining private meetings from the Teams app*

To join a meeting through the Outlook add-in

1. In the Outlook calendar, click the meeting to open the invite.

2. Click **Join Microsoft Teams Meeting**.

Channel Meetings

Channel meetings (see Figure 4-6) are scheduled meetings that occur in a team's channel, based on the topic. Channel meetings offer many benefits. One benefit is that they make it possible to quickly invite everyone from a team to a meeting. Another benefit is that information about the meeting is saved in the channel as an organizational asset. While working in Teams, it is obvious to team members that a meeting is occurring in a channel: a camera icon appears to the right of the channel name. In the channel conversations, a large message is posted when the meeting starts. The message shows each person who has joined the meeting by displaying their profile pictures in a small circle in the top right of the message. At the bottom of the meeting message, you see the chat. Additionally, a timer shows how long the meeting has been taking place.

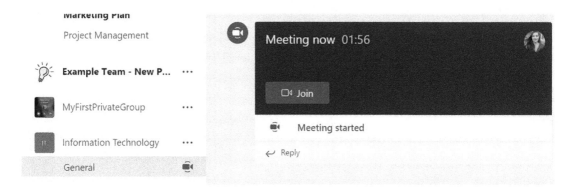

Figure 4-6. *Channel meeting*

Scheduling Channel Meetings

Channel meetings can only be scheduled through the Microsoft Teams app (not with the Outlook add-in). All team members receive an email notification when a channel meeting is scheduled.

Note   After a meeting completes, the total time of the meeting, the meeting attendees, and the chat are saved in the channel automatically.

To schedule a channel meeting

1. Click the meetings icon located on the left in the Microsoft Teams app.

2. Click the **Schedule a meeting** button.

3. Fill out the title, start date and time, and end date and time, at a minimum.

4. Pick a channel from the **Select a channel to meet in** drop-down menu, as seen in Figure 4-7.

5. Click the **Schedule a meeting** button.

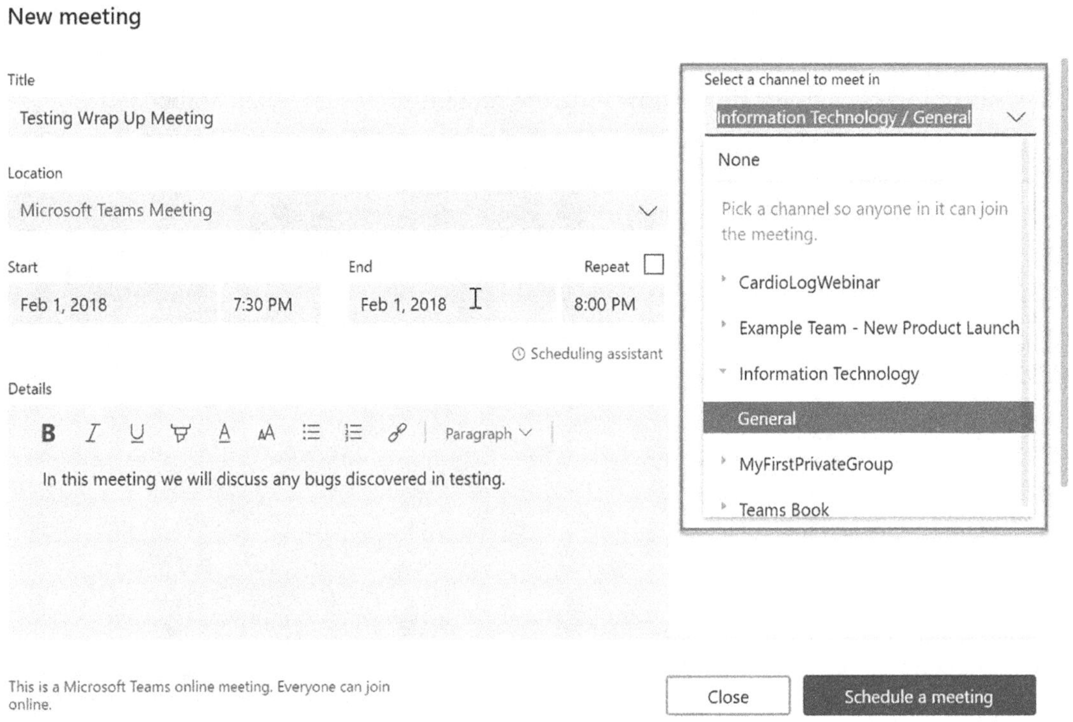

New meeting

Title

Testing Wrap Up Meeting

Location

Microsoft Teams Meeting   ∨

Start   End   Repeat ☐

Feb 1, 2018   7:30 PM   Feb 1, 2018 I   8:00 PM

                                                ⏱ Scheduling assistant

Details

B *I* U̲ ⩒ A̲ AA ☰ ☷ ⊘ | Paragraph ∨ |

In this meeting we will discuss any bugs discovered in testing.

Select a channel to meet in

Information Technology / General   ∨

None

Pick a channel so anyone in it can join
the meeting.

› CardioLogWebinar

› Example Team - New Product Launch

▾ Information Technology

    General

› MyFirstPrivateGroup

› Teams Book

This is a Microsoft Teams online meeting. Everyone can join
online.

[Close]   [Schedule a meeting]

Figure 4-7. Scheduling a channel meeting

Joining a Meeting by Audio Conference

Participants in Microsoft Teams can join meetings by phone while they are on the go. This
is useful when a meeting participant does not have access to the internet. Participants
that have this feature receive dial-in instructions in the Teams meeting invite.

Note   Only meeting participants that have the audio conferencing feature enabled
in Office 365 receive dial-in instructions.

Meeting Agenda

The meeting agenda is a central location that shows you all the upcoming private and
channel meetings that you are invited to. By default, you see all the meetings for the
week. If you click the blocked icon located in the top-right corner of the agenda (see
Figure 4-8), you can change the view to only show meetings for the day.

Figure 4-8. *Meeting agenda*

Meet Now Meetings

Meet Now meetings allow spontaneous meetings with all team members. Meet Now meetings are a great way to quickly share a message or bring a team together in an urgent situation. They are similar to channel meetings in that they are initiated and take place within a channel. When a Meet Now meeting is started, a conversation message is added to the channel that looks the same as it does for channel meetings. The meeting name, attendees, elapsed meeting time, and chat messages are all part of the Meet Now meeting conversation messages. The camera icon to the right of the channel name and the team members' names show that a meeting is happening. One thing different about Meet Now meetings is that the video option is on for the person who initiates the meeting.

To start a Meet Now meeting

1. Click the camera icon located below the text box in the conversations tab of the channel that you want to hold the meeting in (see Figure 4-9).

2. Enter a subject and click the **Meet now** button.

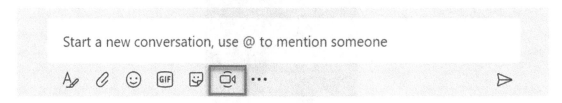

Start a new conversation, use @ to mention someone

Figure 4-9. *Starting a Meet Now meeting*

Note   Entering a subject for a Meet Now meeting is optional, but it is recommended so that team members know the purpose of the meeting.

Meeting Controls for Participants

Participants in Microsoft Teams meetings have control over how they participate in a meeting and what they share. To get the most out of meetings, use of video and voice are recommended. However, participants can choose whether or not they show themselves in a video or use voice. Participants can also choose to share their screen. Microsoft Teams has a feature that allows you to choose which window on your desktop that you want to share, in case you don't want people to see your email or anything else that is personal. The controls for participants are in the middle of the meeting screen, as seen in Figure 4-10. You do not see the controls until you move your mouse into that general area.

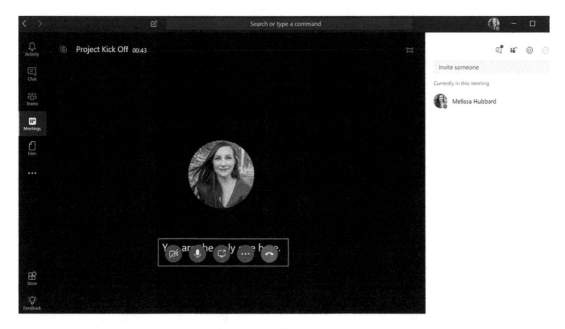

Figure 4-10. *Participant meeting controls*

Muting the Mic

When a participant has their mic open, and there is background noise, it can be very distracting for everyone in the meeting. It is best practice to keep the mic muted unless you are speaking. If you are speaking and no one is responding to you, check your mic because you may have forgotten to unmute yourself!

To mute the mic

1.   Move the mouse to the middle area of the meeting screen.

2.   Click the microphone icon.

To unmute, follow the same instructions. The microphone icon has a slash going through it when muted, as seen in Figure 4-11.

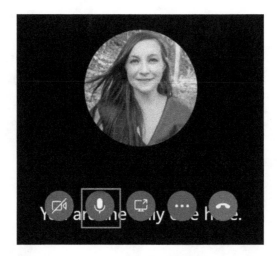

Figure 4-11. *Muting the mic*

Disabling Video

Communicating with other meeting participants is best with video. When people can see your expressions along with hearing you speak, they are the most likely to understand your message. For the times that you do not want others to see you, such as when you aren't in a professional meeting location or you are multitasking, video can easily be disabled.

To disable the video

1.   Move your mouse to the middle area of the meeting screen.

2.   Click the video camera icon, as seen in Figure 4-12.

To turn the video back on, follow the same instructions. If you have a profile picture, it will show when you talk (instead of video).

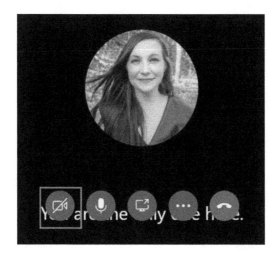

Figure 4-12. *Disabling the Video*

Screen Sharing

Screen sharing is an extremely valuable feature. Common uses of screen sharing are to show presentation slides or to walk participants through some process or work tool. All participants can share their screen except unauthenticated guests not using the Microsoft Teams app.

To screen share

1. Move your mouse to the middle area of the meeting screen.

2. Click the computer screen icon, as seen in Figure 4-13.

3. Choose whether you want to share your desktop or an app. Click the screen or app of choice.

To end screen sharing, click the computer screen icon again.

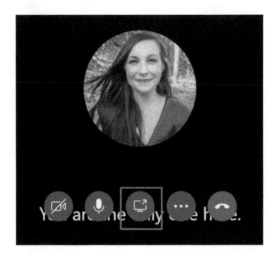

Figure 4-13. *Screen sharing*

Giving Control of the Screen

When a meeting participant is sharing their screen, another participant may need to take control of their screen or application to demonstrate something. A participant can both give control of their screen and request control.

To give control of the screen

1. Click the **Give control** drop-down menu located on the top center of the screen while screen sharing.

2. Select the person's name that you want to give control to.

Multitasking in Teams

Microsoft Teams makes it possible to continue working within the app while also participating in a meeting. Simply click out of the meeting anywhere within the Microsoft Teams application, and the meeting will shrink to a small window located on the top left of the app. To return to the meeting in a full window, click the small meeting window.

Hanging Up a Meeting

To hang up a meeting

1. Move your mouse to the middle area of the meeting screen.

2. Click the red phone icon, as seen in Figure 4-14.

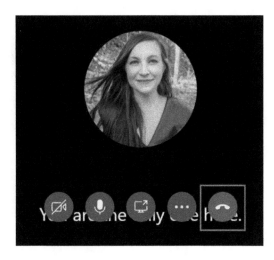

Figure 4-14. *Hanging up a meeting*

Meeting Controls for Organizers

Meeting organizers have controls in place that allow them to make sure that the meeting runs smoothly. Organizers can admit participants into the meeting from the lobby, mute participants, and remove participants.

Admitting Participants from the Lobby

One of the jobs of the meeting organizer is to admit authenticated guests that have joined the meeting from the lobby. Depending on the subject matter of the meeting, it may be very important to carefully review the names of the guests waiting in the lobby. If something sensitive is being discussed, you do not want someone that should not be attending to get into the meeting.

To admit a participant from the lobby

1. Click the check mark to the right of the guest's name, as seen in Figure 4-15.

2. Clicking the X to the right of the person's name rejects the person from joining the meeting.

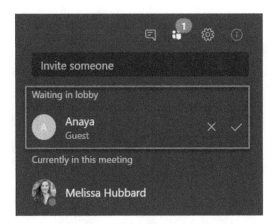

Figure 4-15.   *Admitting participants from the lobby*

Muting Participants

At times, a participant may not realize that they have their mic open, or they may have stepped away from their desk. If your meeting is being disrupted by background noise or someone having a conversation outside of the meeting, the organizer can mute participants. You will know who is making the noise because the meeting tells you who is currently speaking. There is also the option to mute all participants. This is an especially useful feature when there are a large number of attendees in a meeting.

To mute a participant

1. Click the ellipse (...) to the right of the participant's name in the list of people currently in the meeting.

2. Click **Mute participant**, as seen in Figure 4-16.

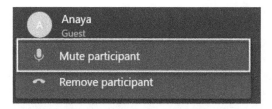

Figure 4-16. *Muting a participant*

The participant will be able to unmute their mic when they want to speak again, but the current distraction is fixed.

Note   To mute all participants, click the **Mute all** link located above the list of people currently in the meeting, as seen in Figure 4-17.

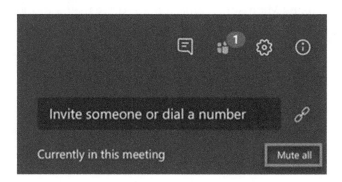

Figure 4-17. *Muting all participants*

Removing Participants

At times, a participant may be too disruptive or is invited in error. In these situations, the meeting organizer can remove a participant.

To mute a participant

1. Click the ellipse (…) to the right of the participant's name in the list of people currently in the meeting.

2. Click **Remove participant**, as seen in Figure 4-18.

Figure 4-18. *Removing a participant*

Summary

In this chapter, we walked through the multiple ways to hold meetings in Teams, as well as the different meeting controls for meeting organizers and participants. The meeting features in Teams are very helpful for driving productivity, especially for teams that are not able to hold meetings in person. When members of an organization realize the value of holding meetings using Microsoft Teams, it helps drive user adoption of the product. More about user adoption of Microsoft Teams is covered in the next chapter.

CHAPTER 5

User Adoption in Teams

Have you seen eyes rolling and heard the moaning when a memo is sent out telling you and your teammates of a new intranet that they will need to use? Have you felt annoyed when you are told by leadership that there is a change to the performance review process and system, which is the third change in two years? If you ask information technology leaders what the biggest challenges of implementing new software are, user adoption will be at the top of the list.

User adoption is when the members of an organization accept and use a new software or tool that has been introduced to their work environment to its fullest extent. Organizations struggle with this for a variety of reasons. People simply do not like to change their work habits once they are a rhythm, even if it will save them time and make their life easier in the long run. This is especially true when they have a high workload or stress at work. It is difficult to switch gears and use a new software or tool when organization members are struggling to meet deadlines or have conflicting priorities. Also, there is often a lack of trust in new software or tools. If an organization has suffered through failed rollouts of software in the past, end users become disenchanted when they hear of something new. This is especially true if many people lost work and/or time, or if this is the perception.

Training can also be an issue in user adoption. Well-intentioned organization members may try to adopt a new software or tool but struggle with how to use it properly. If they can't quickly resolve it, they are likely to go back to old tools or to find work-arounds that do not involve the new software.

Note   User adoption planning is just as important as implementation planning, so do not cut corners. It will not matter how smoothly the technical implementation of Microsoft Teams goes if there is weak user adoption.

© Melissa Hubbard, Matthew J. Bailey 2018
M. Hubbard and M. J. Bailey, *Mastering Microsoft Teams*, https://doi.org/10.1007/978-1-4842-3670-3_5

Many IT professionals have watched these user adoption issues plague their collaboration software rollouts for years. Many lessons have been learned that can be drawn upon to ensure that organizations are successful with Microsoft Teams user adoption.

When to Use What for Collaboration

Yammer an Office 365 tool for enterprise-wide social networking and sharing information. Another relatively new service from Microsoft is Office 365 Groups. Office 365 Groups provide a shared workspace that includes email, conversations, files, and events in which members of a group can collaborate and get work completed via the Outlook client. The important distinction to make here is that Microsoft Teams is a platform with even more features, although in some ways they are connected in the background.

There are many reasons to use Microsoft Teams. Although a single team can have up to 2,500 members, we do not recommend using Microsoft Teams solely for sharing organizational-level announcements and information. Microsoft Teams is not meant to replace an organization's intranet. Knowing when to use which tool can sometimes be a bit confusing. To help guide you a bit more, Figure 5-1 is based on Microsoft's "inner circle/outer circle" reference.

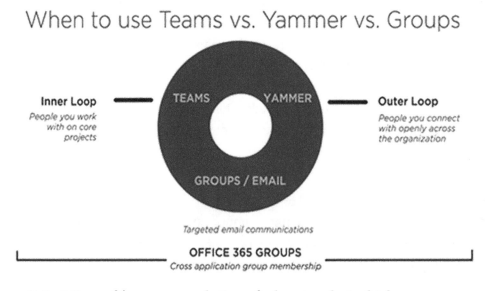

Figure 5-1. *Microsoft's recommendation of when to select which collaboration tool*

Real-World Use Cases

The following are some examples of how Microsoft Teams can be used to maximize the benefits the app has to offer. It is important to remember that every organization is different, and Microsoft Teams may fit into the information technology strategy in various ways.

Use Case 1: Coordinating a New Initiative

A nonprofit organization is starting a new initiative to educate children about healthy eating in impoverished schools. It creates a private team and adds everyone that is working on the initiative as team members. A channel is added for each of the four schools the initiative is targeting. Within those channels, the team members discuss their lessons plans, creation of materials, scheduling, and other topics related to the particular school. They use the documents tab in these channels to store the customized learning materials and forms that they created for each school. The team members that are assigned to each school favorite and follow the channel for that particular school to make sure that they stay up-to-date on all channel activities. The General channel is used to discuss topics that apply to the overall initiative, such as funding and team assignments. A tab is set up showing a Power BI chart displaying metrics on the number of students that have participated in the initiative from each school. The wiki outlines the protocols that should be followed when team members arrive at a school. Team members often use group chat messages to quickly reach a consensus about planning decisions. A sample of the channel structure is seen in Figure 5-2.

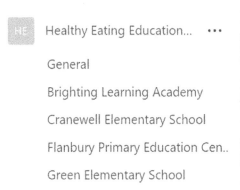

Figure 5-2. *Use Case 1: Coordinating a project with channels*

Use Case 2: Departmental Collaboration

The Human Resources department of a mid-sized company has a private team created for them by the IT department. Channels are set up for the different functions and activities of the department, such as recruitment, benefits, payroll, and training.

The General channel contains a tab for the benefits service that the whole team uses regularly in their work day. The recruitment channel has tabs for a SharePoint list where recruitment possibilities are stored, as well as a tab containing a Microsoft Word document that is regularly referred to for guidance when cold-calling recruits. The training channel is primarily used to discuss the training materials being developed.

Team members use a tab containing a Microsoft Excel document that the organization uses to track employees' mandatory training requirements. The benefits channel stores many documents from benefits vendors that are distributed to staff. During the time of year to shop for benefits plans, the conversations tab is very active. The team holds weekly meetings in the benefits channel to discuss any new updates and issues. The payroll channel is active with team members asking each other questions about their payroll software and resolving time card discrepancies. You can see the channel structure of this use case in Figure 5-3.

Figure 5-3. *Use Case 2: Departmental collaboration with channels*

Use Case 3: Managing IT Projects

A small IT consulting company has 40 staff members spread out in several different countries and who all work from home. They have five large long-term clients for which they provide IT solutions and support. In Microsoft Teams, they have a separate team for each client because they do not want staff members viewing the content of a client they are not working with.

Each team has channels for project management, development, and testing. Project managers use a tab in the project management channel to display the Planner app in Office 365, where they assign and track tasks. They also schedule daily stand-up meetings in Microsoft Teams, track attendance, and ask for updates in the meeting chat.

The testing channels are used by the quality assurance team members. They discuss testing activities and schedules. Also, they contain a tab to a quality log that is in a SharePoint list. The development channels have tabs displaying Visual Studio Team Services, which is a tool the developers use as a code repository and to track bugs. They often hold meetings where they share their screens and do code reviews.

Pilots

Microsoft Teams is a very malleable tool, which enables it to achieve many different business needs for chat, collaboration, and meetings. There are so many different ways that Microsoft Teams can be used, as well as settings and features that can be adjusted. Because of this, it is recommended to roll out Teams on a small scale first. Holding a Teams pilot minimizes risk by providing a way to work out the specifics of your organizational culture, rather than impacting the entire organization.

The following are the benefits of doing a pilot:

- Determines the areas that users struggle with so that training can be the most beneficial

- Analyzes patterns in how the pilot group uses Microsoft Teams

- Receives the pilot group's feedback and turns it into actionable ways to improve the organization's experience with Microsoft Teams

- Excites a group of users who (hopefully) become pioneers and cheerleaders for Microsoft Teams

- Discovers any performance or security issues

- Resolves any technical issues, such as firewall configuration, application incompatibility, or authentication inconveniences that affect user experience

Choose one or a few projects, departments, or initiatives to use Microsoft Teams and provide feedback before it goes to the masses so that you greatly increase the probability of successful user adoption. Elect the right group of people for a pilot is important. Generally, a good mix of skill levels and positive attitudes are the most important characteristics for a pilot group. Using the IT department for your pilot group may not represent how the rest of the organization will use the tool because IT professionals tend to be more knowledgeable about Microsoft Teams and are adept in implementing new software. You also don't want to choose a group that is too busy to provide feedback or use Microsoft Teams to its fullest potential.

The organization's size, culture, and technology skills determine the level of structure needed for the pilot. The training section of this chapter discusses the basic topics that users need to have an understanding of. Providing some form of training to the pilot group before they start will give them the skills to make the most out of the pilot.

At a minimum, there should be a pilot kickoff meeting that outlines the pilot's

- Goals

- Expectations

- Schedule

- Success criteria

User Adoption Tips

User adoption is an art and a science. The most important thing is to have a strategy, but be flexible enough to make adjustments if something isn't working. Your organization may already have lessons learned about user adoption from previous software rollouts that can be drawn upon when rolling out Microsoft Teams. These tips are a great starting point.

Define Your Vision

The first step of having a successful Microsoft Teams implementation is deciding to use it for the right reasons. The key target business scenario for adopting Microsoft Teams is a group of team members working on the same job function or project that need to chat, collaborate, and hold meetings.

Additionally, before rolling out Microsoft Teams, it is a good idea to identify why you are rolling out Microsoft Teams in the first place. Although Microsoft Teams is new and exciting software, adding it because everyone else is, or because it is new, are not necessarily the best reasons to deploy it. Understanding the challenges your users experience in the workplace and how Microsoft Teams can address those challenges helps with adoption. The following are some of the ways that Microsoft Teams can address these challenges:

- Makes remote users feel more connected, as though they are working in the same office

- Saves time by not having to open multiple applications to collaborate with other workers

- Improves the findability of related artifacts by having them in one location

Of course, each organization's reasoning is different, but taking the time to identify the reasons helps you create a foundation for a successful Microsoft Teams implementation.

Communicate the Benefits

Months prior to releasing Microsoft Teams in an organization, start a communications campaign focusing on the benefits to the users. Some organizations have staff members whose main role is to develop and carry out communication strategies. For other organizations, it is sufficient to bring up Microsoft Teams in meetings or to post an announcement on the intranet.

Identify the Right Team Owners

It is crucial to have team owners that are advocates of Microsoft Teams. If there is anyone that was ever an owner or took a special interest in another collaboration tool, such as SharePoint, they may be a good candidate. Team owners interface with team members, and it is important that the owners have a positive attitude and thorough understanding of how Microsoft Teams works. Team owners should feel empowered to make decisions and try new ways to use Microsoft Teams to maximize the benefits. Forcing someone who is too busy to be a team owner, or who is uninterested in being a team owner, is detrimental to user adoption.

Ways Team Owners Can Engage Team Members

The best way for team owners to engage their team members is to set a shining example of how Microsoft Teams should be used. When team owners notice a long group email conversation, they should respond, "Let's take this conversation to Microsoft Teams." Often, team members suggest holding a meeting to discuss something that could be handled in conversations in Microsoft Teams. Team owners can start a conversation in Microsoft Teams and let team members know that time could be saved if the subject is discussed there.

If a team member is slow to start using Microsoft Teams, the team owner can @mention the person in conversations so that they receive notifications and are included in the collaboration efforts. Another great way team owners can support team members is by being available to answer questions. Team members are much more likely to use Microsoft Teams if they have someone to reach out to when they are confused or have questions.

Stop Duplication

A really big turn off for users is when they feel they have to perform a work function twice. This can happen when some users adopt Microsoft Teams but others haven't. An example is if a user uploads a document to a channel in Microsoft Teams and sends a message to a team member asking them to review it. The team member hasn't adopted Microsoft Teams so never reads the message. The user then ends up having to email them the document and ask them again to review it. This is bound to happen during the early stages of a Microsoft Teams release, but it needs to be corrected or there will be a lot of frustration. It may take leadership communicating that it is an expectation that everyone uses Microsoft Teams and reads their messages.

Check in with Users

It is a mistake to release Microsoft Teams to an organization and not frequently touch base with the users to receive feedback and answer any questions. This helps users feel supported and serves as a reminder to use it. Checking in with users is beneficial to increasing user adoption as long as actions are taken to improve user experiences based on feedback. All too often, users are experiencing issues and do not let anyone know because no one asks.

Let the Users Have Fun

The GIFs, stickers, and emojis in Microsoft Teams definitely offer a certain fun factor that most users enjoy. This can assist in fostering a positive culture where team members can express themselves. Unless there is a legitimate reason to disable or limit the GIFs and stickers, leave them be. If the GIFs and stickers are overused or become inappropriate, it may be only a few users that need guidance. If it is a widespread issue, then communicate guidance to all users and make adjustments to the settings if necessary. In Figure 5-4, you can see the authors having fun while writing this book.

Figure 5-4. *Having fun with Microsoft Teams*

Training

Training is an essential part of user adoption. Microsoft Teams is very user-friendly, but even the most tech savvy of organizations should receive some training and guidance. Ideally, training would begin right before Microsoft Teams is rolled out in the organization. Users should also have access to training materials. There needs to be a clear path for users to get questions answered. One idea is a channel in the team that contains training materials, and the conversations tab is for team members to answer questions.

All users should have an understanding of the following concepts:

- How to access Microsoft Teams

- How to use teams and channels

- What tabs and connectors are

- How to chat and contribute to conversations

- How to share and access files

- How to schedule and attend meetings

- How to manage notifications

Team owners have additional duties in Microsoft Teams that they need to be trained in. Ideally, team owners will also be available to answer questions from team members. It is important that team owners understand the differences in what a team owner can do in Microsoft Teams compared to someone in a team member role.

Team owners should have an understanding of these concepts:

- How to create, edit, and delete a team

- How to add team members to a team

- How to manage team settings

Microsoft Teams offers a wide array of training videos within the application. Microsoft realized the importance of proper user training in how to use an application. Although these videos are very helpful and a great improvement over some past software that has been released, they may not be all the information that you need to make accessible to your users. In Chapter 6, you learn that creating a process for users to request a team is a much better idea than just allowing anyone to create a team at any time. As a part of this process, you could add any custom training you feel is necessary for your users before they are allowed to use the team.

Ongoing Monitoring and Improvement

Adoption isn't always thought of as an ongoing process. Unfortunately, many organizations feel they do not have the resources or do not understand the impact of not implementing ongoing adoption. Like all software, the more it is used, the more you will find ways to improve how you interact with it. Over time, you may find that the software *stops* being used. There are almost always legitimate reasons why this occurs. It is important that someone is responsible for addressing the issue and resolving it to ensure long-term success with the application.

Microsoft understands the need for ongoing monitoring as part of the overall adoption of Teams. Microsoft introduced usage reports in the Office 365 admin center for most of its products. *To access these reports, you need to have your Office 365 administrator compile them for you or give you an admin role in the Office 365 admin center to allow you to create these reports yourself.*

At the moment, there are two specific reports that can be processed for Microsoft Teams:

- Microsoft Teams usage activity

- Microsoft Teams device usage

The *usage activity* report has Activity and Users tabs to surface information via a graph. In addition to this, there is detailed information on when the last time a user was active in a team, and the number of channel messages, chats, calls, and meetings each user has performed. From this data, you extract a number of different ideas on what might be happening in case long-term user adoption starts to fall off.

The good thing about these reports is that by listing the individual user's activity, you can quickly see which users might have been very active but suddenly their activity dropped. If a problem with long-term usage arises, you know which users to ask first about the problem. An example of this report is shown Figure 5-5.

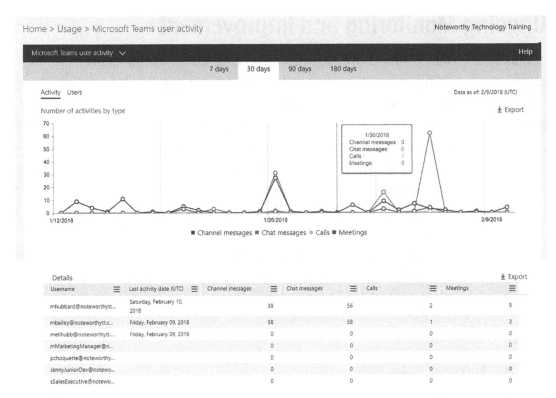

Figure 5-5. *Sample usage report for Microsoft Teams from the Office 365 admin center*

You (or your Office 365 administrator) have access to the Microsoft Teams Device Usage report. One benefit of this report is that it helps you realize the number of users accessing Microsoft Teams via a mobile device. Also, if a specific mobile device's statistics suddenly trend downward, you can investigate the issue. Earlier in the book, we mentioned that mobile devices do not have all the same functionalities that the client and web interfaces have. If you see a downward trend in a specific mobile operating system (not due to it becoming extinct, such as with Palm), the mobile app may have presented an issue for users that you are not aware of. An example of this report is shown in Figure 5-6.

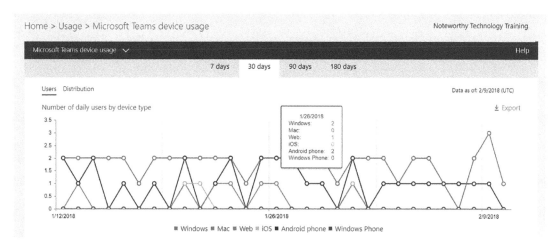

Figure 5-6. *Sample usage by device report for Teams from the Office 365 admin center*

Summary

Hopefully, the biggest takeaway from this chapter is that adoption and long-term success with Microsoft Teams in your organization is not something that you should overlook or think will take just a small amount of time. It may not be easy to implement all of these strategies and ideas or find stakeholders to take on the responsibility to own them, but at least you will know that if you do not perform the tasks at hand, your odds of success will be a lot less than those who have. In the next chapter, we discuss how to govern Microsoft Teams within your organization. User adoption and governance go hand in hand, because if your deployment of Microsoft Teams lacks governance, then performance and functionality suffers, which ultimately turns off your users.

CHAPTER 6

Governance

Governance goes hand in hand with user adoption. Having a well-thought-out governance plan ensures that Microsoft Teams is managed and used in the way it was intended. Users will adopt Microsoft Teams if it is well-governed and useful to them. A solid governance plan ensures that the user experience remains positive and that organization assets are stored and used properly. The biggest selling point of Microsoft Teams is that it improves the speed and ease of collaboration by providing one location where teammates can interact, share content, and conduct meetings. However, the benefits will only be realized if time is spent planning the administration and management of the service prior to making it available to your users. Without a governance plan, there are pitfalls that will negate these benefits.

This chapter discusses the essential areas of governance for Microsoft Teams to consider and offer practical advice. Real-world examples and explanations help you build a governance plan that ensures that content is secure and that Microsoft Teams is convenient and easy to use, thus driving user adoption.

Creating Your Own Plan

Creating your own governance plan for Microsoft Teams should, at the very least, include the following items:

- How to organize the structure of your team (this could be different for each team you create)

- How to allow people to request or create a new team (a process for creating Teams)

- How to determine if there should be a new team created

© Melissa Hubbard, Matthew J. Bailey 2018
M. Hubbard and M. J. Bailey, *Mastering Microsoft Teams*, https://doi.org/10.1007/978-1-4842-3670-3_6

- Understanding options to archive old or unused teams

- Features and organizational settings

Now let's go into more detail for each bullet point so that you can create your own governance plan.

Organizational Structure for Teams and Channels

Microsoft Teams can easily become unmanageable if it is rolled out with the default settings, and users have no guidance. By default, all users can create new teams and channels. One parallel that many IT professionals can draw upon is the structure of SharePoint. Before the importance of governance was realized, many users were given access to create new sites at their discretion. Without proper training, planning, and strategizing about when to create new sites, there quickly became an uncontrollable environment. The lack of governance harmed user adoption of SharePoint; let's use the lessons learned to avoid this happening with Microsoft Teams.

It is very important to analyze your organization's work functions, departments, products, initiatives, and/or projects to strategize how to lay out teams and channels. A key point to remember is that permissions can only be set at the team level. Until Microsoft releases secure channels, all content in channels is open and available to all members of the team that the channel is part of.

Tip   When strategizing the organizational structure of teams and channels, it is very important to consider who should have access to what content.

Figure 6-1 shows an example of an organizational structure where a team is created for each major department, and including each office that falls under the department with a channel.

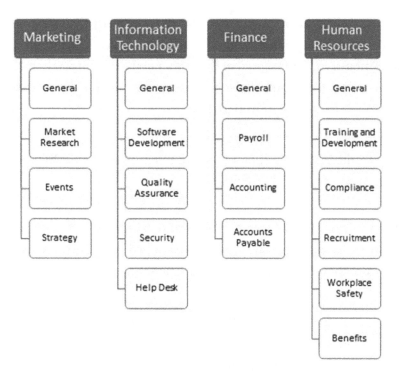

Figure 6-1. *Teams organization by department*

As you can see, the Information Technology department has a team with channels for the Help Desk, Software Development, Quality Assurance, and Security offices. The General channel is used for department-wide communication and file sharing. Each office uses their channel for communication and collaboration. This organizational structure makes sense in theory, but if the Security office is communicating about confidential topics in their conversations tab, all the other offices will be able to read it. In a situation like this, each office needs its own team.

Note   Being able to restrict permissions at the channel level is a highly anticipated piece of functionality for Teams. Microsoft is looking into adding it, but no date is set at this time.

Now imagine if all of the offices were already heavily using their channel in the Information Technology team by having conversations, holding meetings, and uploading files. After four months, it is realized that the team needs to be broken up so that each office can have its own team. But, all the conversations and meeting information from the offices' channels cannot be moved to their teams.

Note   Conversations and meeting content cannot be moved from one team to another or from one channel to another.

The only option for the offices to see their content in the Information Technology team is to leave the team active. This can lead to confusion and error because the offices may accidently use their old channel instead of their new team.

Tip   If you have to leave a team that is no longer used, but team members still need to access the existing content, rename the team and add a description to indicate that there should be nothing new added. For example, "Information Technology team—READ ONLY." In the description, let users know which team they should be using instead. You can also consider using the archiving functionality found under the "gear" icon in the bottom left corner of your Teams interface, then select the team you would like to archive.

Figure 6-2 shows an organization that has organized teams by project. It is common for organizations to create a team for every project, client, or case that they work on. This is different than organizing by department because there is usually a definitive start and end in these scenarios. Having this structure makes sense for when there are different people working on every project, client, or case, especially if they need to invite external guest users to collaborate with. If a law firm is using Microsoft Teams to collaborate on files and hold conversations about a case, they may want to invite the client to view files in Teams and discuss the case. It is important that they only have access to their own case, not that of others. A separate team per case is the only way to achieve this.

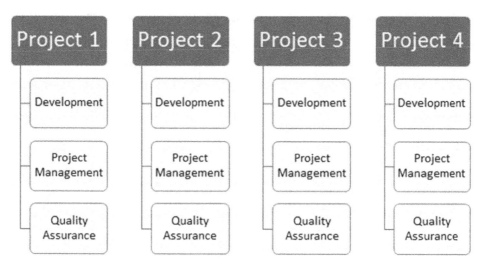

Figure 6-2. *Teams organization by project*

There is no one blueprint for the Microsoft Teams organizational structure that can be used for all organizations. Not properly planning how teams and channels will be organized can severely damage user adoption. It can also put an organization at risk of having sensitive or private content accessed by the wrong people. An analysis of the different work functions of an organization and gaining insight into who is sharing and collaborating on different types of content will help you plan for success. As discussed in Chapter 5, holding a pilot prior to the rollout to the entire organization empowers you in this analysis.

Process for Creating and Managing Teams

Planning the team's organizational structure is the first step. No matter how well you plan, governing the team's organizational structure is an ongoing duty. The next step is to decide how new teams are created and the process to manage it.

Restricting Who Can Create Teams

By default, everyone can create a team. This has both pros and cons. Allowing everyone to be able to create a team allows for fluidity of work and an agile approach for organizations. Small organizations that are technologically savvy may be able to get away with leaving the default team creation setting by providing guidance on when it is appropriate to create a new team.

For medium and large-sized organizations, the default team creation setting can be problematic. With too many cooks in the kitchen, it is inevitable that a team is created in error or for inappropriate reasons. If it becomes confusing for users as to which team or channel to use for different content, user adoption will suffer. To help determine if a formal team creation process should be implemented at your organization, we list the pros and cons of each in Table 6-1.

Table 6-1. *Advantages and Disadvantages of Having a Formal Teams Request Process in an Organization*

Without a team creation governance process	With a team creation governance process
Promotes adoption and usage	Could limit user adoption
Allows users to make a team what they want it to be	Might restrict the ways users can interact and utilize teams
Creates massive sprawl with difficulties managing and taking up storage space	Prevents "teams sprawl," which save sharePoint and other services storage space
Doesn't follow naming conventions	Allows for understandable naming conventions
Possible issues with classification and the types of data being stored in the team	Allows for classification and tracking information about the team
Allows for "inappropriate language" in a name	Prevents users from creating teams named "inappropriately"
Hard to monitor decommissioning and retention	Allows monitoring to know when to decommission or how long to retain a team
Prevents users from agreeing to a terms of service or required training	Can affect other office 365 applications that rely on groups (planner)
Hard to determine what teams you have in your environment (may change)	Allows IT administrators to manage and monitor teams in the organization
Doesn't guarantee an administrator is an owner of a team	Allows you to place an administration group as a team owner
Allows for duplicate team names, which can create confusion for everyone	Prevents duplicate naming

Note   Team members can only be restricted to create channels at the team level. There is no setting in the Office 365 admin center to restrict channel permissions.

As you can see in Table 6-1, most reasoning leans toward implementing a team creation and governance process at an organization. To restrict team creation, an Office 365 administrator needs to run PowerShell commands. One issue with this is that to restrict someone from creating a new team, you have to restrict them from creating a new group in Office 365. This is because when you create a new team, it creates a group. Restricting someone from creating a group also prevents them from creating a team. Obviously, if there is a strong business need for everyone to be able to create groups or Planners in Office 365, you will not be able to restrict them from creating teams.

Note   In order to restrict someone from creating teams, you need to restrict them from creating groups in Office 365.

Process for Creating Teams

If the decision is made to restrict who can create a team, you need to determine a process for how teams are created. There are several options for how this can be handled. What is best can be vastly different from one organization to another.

If the creation of new teams is restricted to a small group of collaboration specialists or IT professionals, users will need a quick and easy process to request new teams. If the process is not clear, or is cumbersome or takes too long, users will find work-arounds to get their jobs done. They could begin using an existing team inappropriately to collaborate on content unrelated to the rest of the Teams' content or they could begin collaborating in a different tool outside of Teams. Once a group of people gets in a work rhythm, it is difficult to change their habits and bring them back to using Teams.

If an organization already has a well-established ticketing system, this may be the best option. It is imperative that end users clearly know how to specifically request a new team. Teams-related requests and questions need to be quickly routed to the collaboration specialists or IT professionals that specialize in Teams. Open lines of communication between those that create the teams and the end users requesting them are necessary.

If an organization does not have an existing ticketing or help desk system, some mechanism for users to request a team is needs to be developed. One suggestion is to use a SharePoint list that everyone in the organization has access to. Figure 6-3 shows an example of a SharePoint list form to request a new team. There should be fields for users to enter the name of the team that they are requesting. It is also important that they provide a reason for needing the team. This helps determine if the team is actually necessary. Team owners of the new team should be included in the request. Also, it is important to find out if external guest users will be part of the proposed team.

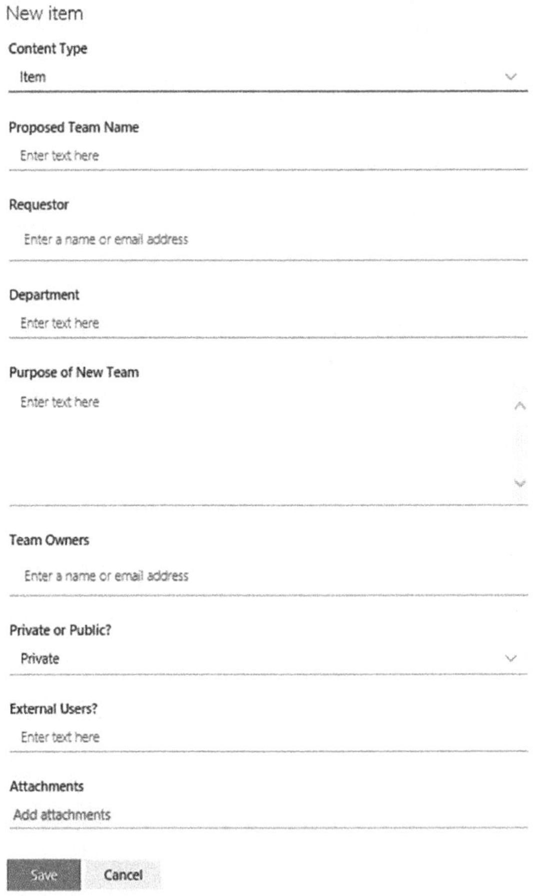

Figure 6-3. Example SharePoint form allowing users to request a new team

Because there are so many different ways that an organization could implement a Teams creation process, in the next section, we explain many of the concepts you could use as a process. There is no magic answer on which process to select. Evaluating the pros and cons of each and matching them to your organization's needs will help you decide which option to pursue.

Teams Creation Options

In this section, we present the options and their pros and cons.

No Team Creation Process

Just "flipping the switch" to turn on Microsoft Teams without any planning or consideration is not an option for most organizations. Unless you have no concerns about the data, we do not advise taking this approach. Noting this, the following states the pros and cons.

Pros

This approach promotes the greatest short-term adoption possibilities, requires little planning or training, and is the fastest to implement.

Cons

The negative consequences of this process are great if you have any need to retain, organize, sort, manage, or reuse your data over a period of time. Later in this chapter, we explain many of the negative effects the process could have.

Team Request Reviewed by Admin or Help Desk

One scenario of a team creation process is implementing a team request process in which a SharePoint list is created for users to submit. An admin, help desk, or IT teams specialist reviews the requests and then creates the team if it is approved.

Pros

The pros of this solution are that it is quick to implement, and there is no additional cost for the organization. Configuration of the SharePoint list could prevent users from submitting a duplicate team name.

Cons

This process requires a human to process each request, which takes time and resources. It also requires you to turn off the ability to create groups for your users and only allow certain persons to create new groups and teams.

Placing Teams Requestors in a Security Group

This approach is another recommended by Microsoft. It could be considered a "meet us in the middle" idea. To implement it, you need your Office 365 administrator to create a security group and only place persons you trust and request in this group. You could ensure that the users have completed training before placing them in this group.

Pros

The pros of this approach are that it frees up time for your IT administrators or help desk by letting trusted users create teams themselves. It also allows those persons to create other related Office 365 applications such as Planners, Yammer groups, and Office 365 groups without further interaction from others.

Cons

This process doesn't guarantee that the people you place in the security group will follow all of your rules. If you have naming conventions, or you want to prevent duplicate names, or you want to restrict the number of teams created due to space and organizational requirements, the users may not abide by the rules.

SharePoint Request List that Triggers a Flow

If you looking for an idea that completely restricts users from creating teams (and any other groups-related applications), this concept is the least programmatic way to accomplish the task. It requires setting up a SharePoint list, which you program to perform any checks that you need before the user submits the list item. Upon the list item being submitted, you trigger a flow that uses the REST API to create a team and then notify your users that the team has been created.

Pros

The advantages of this approach are controlling the number, naming, and frequency of new teams. It also requires a bit less programming than the upcoming final suggestion. It is almost immediate and doesn't require your users to wait for the new team to be created.

Cons

The disadvantages of this approach are that it takes time to create and requires someone who has some technical knowledge. It also requires that your organization has approved the flow to use, and it could end up with additional costs if you have run a very large number of requests. Finally, if you have any needs to customize, the components that create a team (i.e., making alterations to the SharePoint site collection to disable external sharing), you will not be able to do so. The restriction that users have to request any application that is group-based also applies.

SharePoint Request List with PowerShell or Code

This idea is the most intricate of any we have discussed. However, if you are in a very rigid organization that demands structure, governance, and control, this approach will suit you the best. The idea starts with a user requesting a team from a SharePoint list, and then either a scheduled task on a Windows server or Azure Functions processes the list items, creates the team, and notifies the requestor.

Pros

The advantage of this method is that it controls your team down to the greatest detail. You could customize your team (within the parameters that Microsoft allows) to appear in a certain way, or to have certain users in it. You could also alter attached components, such as SharePoint site collection sharing settings. If you need to track other information about the team, or to create an annual review process, it can also be done.

Cons

The downside of this approach is that it requires a skilled programmer to create. You also need either an Azure account or a Windows server to run the code on. If you choose to set the code on a schedule, your users will experience a delay before they can use the team. The restriction that users must request any application that is group-based also applies.

If all of these ideas seem too time-consuming and difficult, you can search the Internet for a third-party application that automates it. These products usually cost a great deal and need to be thoroughly investigated before purchasing.

Determining If a New Team Should Be Created

When reviewing a request for a new team, there are a few factors that you should consider in determining whether the team should be created. Primarily, you want to make sure that you avoid duplication by creating a team that already exists. You also want to avoid creating too many teams. Duplication makes it confusing and frustrating for end users. Having a large number of teams creates a hassle for users that are receiving too many notifications and having to switch between teams all day to get work done. If external guest users need to be included on a team, a new team will be needed. The reason is that, typically, external guests are not able to access any team content outside of the work they are performing. Even if the proposed new team could be a channel under an existing team, if external guests shouldn't be able to access the rest of the team channels, a new team has to be created.

When deciding if a new Team should be created, as yourself the following questions:

- Does a team or channel already exist for the same department, initiative, project, case, or account?

- Does a team already exist that has the same members as the proposed team?

- Are external guest team members going to be included?

Roles and Responsibilities

As with any process or system, assigning roles and responsibilities is essential. With Teams, there are primary roles that need to be assigned and communicated to make sure that there is accountability. These roles are decision maker, Office 365 administrator, team owner, and team member.

Decision Maker

There are decisions regarding Teams that need to be made on an ongoing basis. This includes decisions about implementation, configuration, integration with other applications, and processes for creating teams and channels. If an organization decides to limit who can create teams, the decision maker may be in charge of determining whether a team should be created or not. Many large organizations have created governance boards to provide technical leadership and make decisions regarding the use of collaboration tools and their maintenance. We have witnessed SharePoint governance boards kill collaboration and user adoption due to taking too long to make decisions and for micromanaging SharePoint to the point that it was unusable.

When leadership and IT staff, who are usually part of these boards, are too busy or are uninterested in being involved, it slows down collaboration and thus hurts user adoption. In some cases, an official governance board is necessary due to an organizational policy, or the governance board model is successful for decision making on other collaboration tools.

Another option for decision making is to designate specialists to facilitate and expedite collaboration and serve as the liaison between end users, team owners, and Office 365 administrators. These collaboration specialists should have thorough knowledge of Teams, as well as any other collaboration tools that the organization uses. A collaboration specialist ensures that questions and requests are handled promptly.

Office 365 Administrator

Office 365 administrators have access to the Microsoft Teams tenant-wide settings. It is their job to provide technical administration guidance and support. They are also responsible for any performance-related issues experienced when using Microsoft Teams.

Team Owner

Team owners have the important responsibility of leading a team. Team owners monitor the content and make sure that it is appropriate and productive. Team owners also have several settings that they can change for the team, and directly impact the experience team members have when working in the team. Teams allows for up to ten team owners per team. In most cases, we recommend having at least two team owners, but not more than four. Having any more than this will most likely lead to confusion and aggravation. Team owners should always stay in close communication with one another so that everyone is on the same page, especially when changing settings, which are discussed later in this chapter. Team members always need to know who the team owners are so that they know where to go for a first line of support and questions.

Team Member

Team members can be part of one or many teams. Anyone in an organization assigned a Teams license can be a team member. Team members are responsible for staying current on their work. They have the responsibility to discuss and work on the appropriate content for the team and channel. They also need to understand how to follow and favorite teams and channels so that their notifications are effective.

Feature Review

Remarkably, much of the functionality in Microsoft Teams can be changed and customized. Some of the feature customization is done at the team level and some at the organizational level. Team owners have the ability to customize their team's features and member permissions in the team settings. The vast power team owners have to shape the user experience is just one more reason that it is critical to choose the right team owners and train them.

Office 365 administrators can use tenant-wide settings to change and customize the features for all teams. Some settings can be set at both the team level and the organizational level. It is important to know that the tenant-wide settings always take priority over the team settings.

Note   You can customize Teams features at both the organizational level and the team level, but the organizational settings always take precedence.

Organizational Settings

An organization's Teams experience and features can be customized using the Office 365 admin center tenant-wide settings. Every organization has unique business needs and scenarios. Teams is built in a way that much of the functionality can be enabled or disabled in an a la carte fashion. Holding a pilot helps establish which features should be enabled or disabled in an organization. Once Teams is rolled out to everyone in the organization, everyone becomes accustomed to the functionalities. End users will be unhappy if features get removed after they have already started using them. For this reason, it is important for Teams administrators to perform a review of the feature settings in the Office 365 admin center.

To review Teams tenant-wide settings in the admin center

1. Click **Settings**, and then click **Services & add-ins**, as shown in Figure 6-4.

2. Select **Microsoft Teams** from the list.

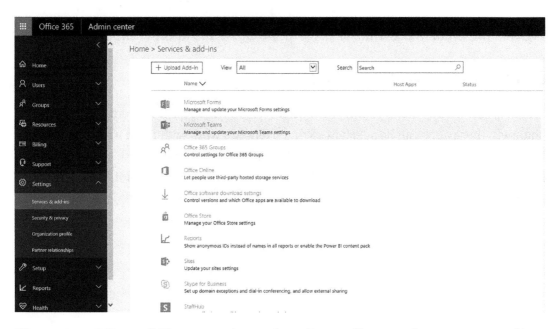

Figure 6-4. *Microsoft Teams service settings. Depending on when you are reading this, this option may have been moved to the Skype for Business and Microsoft Teams admin center in Office 365.*

Email Integration

Since by default every channel is given an email address that anyone can send emails to, Microsoft provides a way to disable or limit them. Office 365 administrators can restrict everyone from being able to email all channels. They can also set it so that only people from certain email domains can send channel emails.

We suggest only disabling email to every channel if there is a legitimate need. When emails are sent to the channel email address, they show as messages in the conversations tab, and team members can respond there. This reduces the number of group emails. You may want to limit who can email the channel if you start getting spammed, or emails become distracting or irrelevant to the work (see Figure 6-5).

Figure 6-5. *Email integration settings in the Office 365 admin center*

External Apps and Cloud Storage

Microsoft Teams has the capability to connect with other apps. When creating tabs in channels, these apps can be selected so that users can work with them without having to leave the Microsoft Teams app. Office 365 admins can disable the use of any external apps, as seen in Figure 6-6. They can also pick and choose which apps should be allowed. You can also enable side-loading apps.

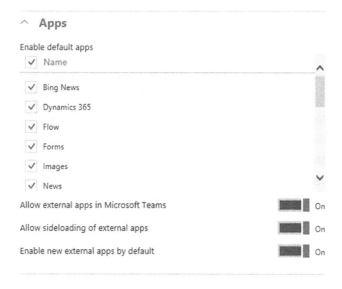

Figure 6-6. *Apps settings in the Office 365 admin center*

Cloud Storage

Cloud storage options outside of Office 365, such as Google Drive or Dropbox, can be configured to allow uploading and sharing files. Office 365 administrators can choose to disable all cloud storage options or to only keep some enabled. We see an example of these settings in Figure 6-7.

Figure 6-7. *Cloud storage options in the Teams settings in the Office 365 admin center*

Messaging

There are many messaging options that the Office 365 administrator can change. Private chat can be completely disabled. The messaging experience can be customized by changing options for memes, stickers, and GIFs. The content rating can be changed if posting explicit content is a concern. The important messaging settings are the ones that impact message editing and deletion. By default, users can edit and delete all of their own messages. There is a setting (that is not enabled by default) that allows team owners to delete all messages, as seen in Figure 6-8. There may be a need to turn this on if there are a lot of "fluff" messages in a team. This setting should be enabled with caution, and team owners should receive training and guidance on this.

Figure 6-8. *Messaging settings in the Teams in the Office 365 admin center*

Calls and Meetings

Private, channel, and ad hoc meetings can all be disabled. If an organization already has a method for holding virtual meetings that users have adopted, and it is working well, it may be a good idea to disable meetings in Teams in order to avoid confusion. An organization may have issues with allowing video and screen sharing in meetings if there are any bandwidth or security policies prohibiting it. These options can be disabled, as seen in Figure 6-9. Private calling is another option that can be disabled if necessary.

Figure 6-9. *Calls and meeting settings in the Office 365 admin center*

External Users

Teams allows external users to collaborate with team members. There is a common business need to invite clients, subcontractors, vendors, and consultants to view team files and hold conversations within Teams. Many agencies have privacy concerns about allowing external users within Teams. To keep external users out of Teams, Office 365 administrators can select Guest as the license type, and then turn off Teams as the users of that type (see Figure 6-10).

Figure 6-10. *Preventing external users from accessing a team in the Office 365 admin center*

Team-Level Settings

Team owners can customize how their team is used by changing the team settings. Team member and guest permissions can be changed, as well as the ability to mention teams and channels, and the "fun" settings, which include emojis, memes, and GIFs. These settings do not impact any other teams.

It is important that team members know to only change these settings if there is a need. Team owners should communicate any setting changes to end users so that they are not surprised when they are unable to do something.

To review team settings

1. Click the ellipse (...) to the right of the team name.

2. Click **Manage team**.

3. Click **Settings**, as seen in Figure 6-11.

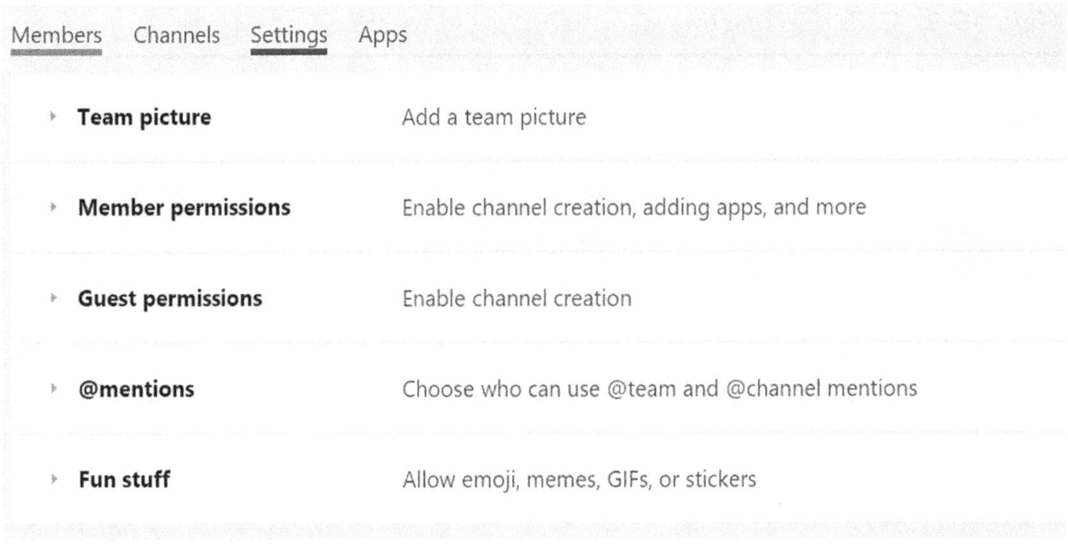

Members   Channels   Settings   Apps

> **Team picture**   Add a team picture

> **Member permissions**   Enable channel creation, adding apps, and more

> **Guest permissions**   Enable channel creation

> **@mentions**   Choose who can use @team and @channel mentions

> **Fun stuff**   Allow emoji, memes, GIFs, or stickers

Figure 6-11. *Team settings*

Member Permissions

Team owners have a set of permissions that they can remove for team members. Permissions are set for all team members. There is no way to grant some team members different permissions than other team members, except for guest members. For large or not technologically savvy teams, we recommend removing the ability to create, update, delete, and restore channels, apps, tabs, and connectors. These actions should be performed at the team owner's discretion. Some organizations may way to remove the permissions of team members to delete and/or edit their messages. Be very cautious about changing these settings because team members will be much less likely to use the conversation functionality in Teams if the know they can't edit typos or delete messages written in error or that they change their mind about. Figure 6-12 illustrates these settings.

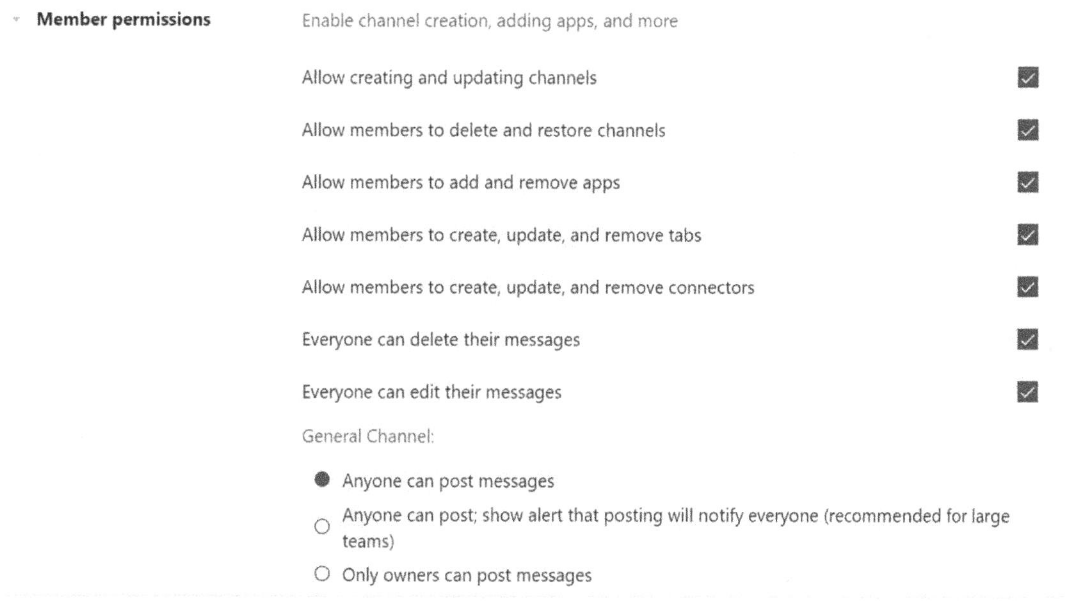

Member permissions   Enable channel creation, adding apps, and more

Allow creating and updating channels   ☑

Allow members to delete and restore channels   ☑

Allow members to add and remove apps   ☑

Allow members to create, update, and remove tabs   ☑

Allow members to create, update, and remove connectors   ☑

Everyone can delete their messages   ☑

Everyone can edit their messages   ☑

General Channel:

◉ Anyone can post messages

○ Anyone can post; show alert that posting will notify everyone (recommended for large teams)

○ Only owners can post messages

Figure 6-12. *Member permissions settings*

Guest Permissions

There is the ability to grant guest team members permissions for creating, updating, and deleting channels. By default, this is disabled (see Figure 6-13), because there are few situations where guests need or should have this control.

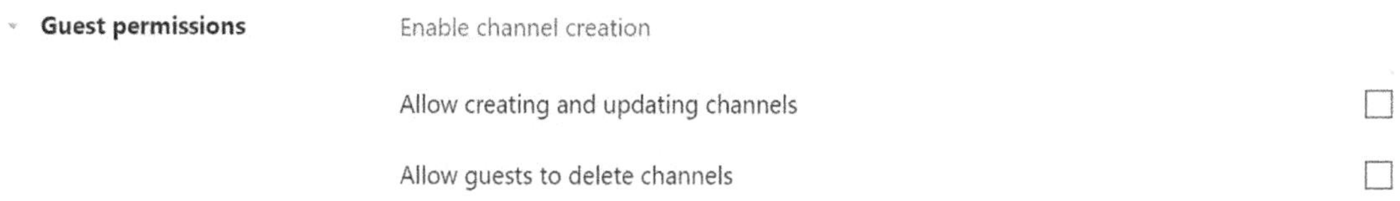

Guest permissions   Enable channel creation

Allow creating and updating channels   ☐

Allow guests to delete channels   ☐

Figure 6-13. *Guest permission settings*

Email Integration

Email settings are configurable on a per channel basis, as seen in Figure 6-14. It is possible to restrict only team members or email addresses from within certain domains so as to be able to email the channel address. Changing the email settings for only a few channels confuses end users, so these settings should only be touched if there is a specific business reason.

Get email address

See <u>advanced settings</u> for more options.

> Media Marketing Plans - Example Team - New Product Launch <971f3c96.notewort

🗑 Remove email address

○   Only members of this team

●   Only email sent from these domains (preset by tenant admin):

> cameronsoft.onmicrosoft.com

| Close | Copy |

Figure 6-14. *Channel email settings*

Team and Channel Mentions

Both teams and channels can be mentioned in conversations, as seen in Figure 6-15. The main point of mentions is that they kick off notifications. A mention of a team sends notifications to everyone on the team. A mention of a channel sends notifications to everyone that follows the channel.

A common complaint about Teams is that there are too many notifications, and so people stop paying attention to them. A team owner may want to disable team and channel mentions if team members are overwhelmed with notifications.

Figure 6-15. *@mentions*

Memes, GIFs, and Stickers Settings

Memes, GIFs, and stickers can be disabled by the team owner. Team owners can also set a content filter to remove anything inappropriate. One scenario where team owners may want to disable the "fun stuff" (see Figure 6-16), is if there are guest members that are clients or customers. Also, if the team is overusing memes, GIFs, and stickers, and don't respond to guidance to minimize their use from the team owner, they may have to resort to completely disabling them.

Fun stuff	Allow emoji, memes, GIFs, or stickers	
	Giphy	
	Enable Giphy for this team	☑
	Filter out inappropriate content using one of the setting below:	
	Moderate ⌄ ⓘ	
	Stickers and memes	
	Enable stickers and memes	☑
	Custom Memes	
	Allow memes to be uploaded	☑

Figure 6-16. Fun stuff

Summary

In this chapter, we reviewed some of the best practices and questions you should ask when a new team is requested. As you can see, there is quite a bit to take into consideration for a proper Microsoft Teams rollout. One bright note, though, is that once you have taken the time to set this up, each corresponding team should flow easily and have a greater chance for adoption.

In the following chapter, we discuss how your organization can gain even more value from Teams by automating business processes using Microsoft Flow and bots.

CHAPTER 7

Automating Business Processes in Teams

In the modern workplace, the automation of business processes and information gathering is becoming more and more commonplace. If a task at work is routine, simple, and repetitive, and involves data entry or searching for information, it is likely a good candidate for business process automation. With Microsoft Teams being a digital workspace that is meant to serve as a catalyst for communication, collaboration, decision making, and creativity, it makes sense to automate as many tasks as possible so that the focus is on bringing the team to the next level of success. Microsoft Teams allows data from third-party cloud-based applications to be leveraged, so the possibilities for business process automation are vast. Business process automation can be achieved in Microsoft Teams using bots and Microsoft Flow.

What Are Bots?

Since Microsoft Teams is a chat-based application, it isn't surprising that you are able to automate some business processes by chatting with a bot. A *bot* is a program that is configured to send predefined messages and decision prompts to end users, which help them to streamline and automate processes. Microsoft Teams offers a platform for team members to interact with intelligent bots in both natural conversations in chat and through specific commands, depending on the bot installed. Bots in Microsoft Teams connect with cloud services. For the most part, bots are built to quickly run simple and repetitive tasks that would take a person much longer to complete. Bots in Microsoft Teams connect with cloud services. They are built by developers using the Microsoft Bot Framework, which allows them to easily connect with Microsoft Teams and the App Store.

© Melissa Hubbard, Matthew J. Bailey 2018
M. Hubbard and M. J. Bailey, *Mastering Microsoft Teams*, https://doi.org/10.1007/978-1-4842-3670-3_7

In Microsoft Teams, bots are initiated in chat messages or in conversation messages in channels; but depending on the bot installed, it may only work in one or the other. When you send a bot a message, it usually sends instructions on what functionality it has to offer. Figure 7-1 shows examples of the bots available in Teams. Some of the apps have other components, such as a tool that can be used in a tab.

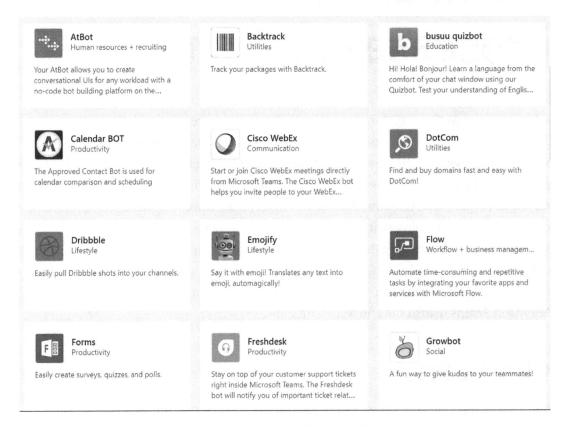

Figure 7-1. Examples of apps with bots available in Teams

Note   The list of bots available in Microsoft Teams is constantly changing as new bots are developed.

What Bots Can Do

Microsoft Teams comes with a bot called the T-Bot, which you can chat with to get information. When Teams is opened for the first time, T-Bot sends a message with instructions on how to interact with it. Figure 7-2 shows the T-Bot, which is a great example of how Microsoft Teams' bots work and what they are capable of.

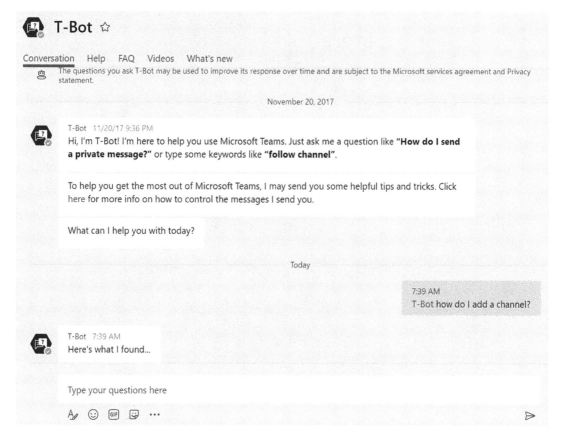

Figure 7-2. *How to use the T-Bot*

Bots in Microsoft Teams connect users with cloud services, and then leverage that cloud service's functionality to perform basic jobs in Teams when you chat with them and give them commands. Bots help Microsoft Teams users with job duties such as scheduling meetings or events, taking polls to gather information from team members, and managing team tasks. In some cases, you may find one bot that does everything you need to automate your business process. Otherwise, it may be necessary to install and combine the functionality of two or more bots. Although apps in the Microsoft Teams store are organized into the categories of Analytics and BI, Developer and IT, Education, Human Resources, Productivity, Project Management, Sales and Support, and Social and Fun, the three main functions that bots are performing are scheduling, task management, and polling. Figure 7-3 shows how apps are organized in the Microsoft Teams App Store.

Figure 7-3. *Organization of apps in the Microsoft Teams App Store*

Scheduling

Scheduling meetings can be a time-consuming task that bots in Teams can assist with. Some examples of how bots can organize meetings are by syncing calendars of team members and showing available times to pick from, polling attendees to vote on the best meeting time, scheduling a meeting and sending out meeting invites, and even providing a list of meeting rooms to book based on which are available.

Although we know meetings can be held in Teams, some organizations that use other products for meetings can disable this feature. Many common meetings services have bots in Teams, so when using the bot, team members are able to create meetings within these services.

Task Management

Bots in Microsoft Teams can assist project managers with tasks such as collecting daily status reports from team members. Reminders to complete status reports can be automatically sent by a bot, and then team members can respond with their status, which is added to a report that can be viewed by the project manager. Reminders to team members can be configured based on when they are due.

There are also bots that can track and manage documents and tasks through their life cycles. Task-based time tracking is also possible within Microsoft Teams using a bot. Project management business processes that involve collecting information, tracking, and reminders can be automated with bots.

Polling

There are bots in Microsoft Teams that have polling capabilities. Polling is a simple way to get feedback from team members by providing them a predefined list of choices that they can select from. Team members can be automatically notified in Microsoft Teams when there is a new poll. The bot consolidates the responses, allowing for the results to be analyzed. Although this functionality may seem trivial, it can be extremely powerful and a huge time-saver when trying to seek the opinions of team members when making a decision.

How to Add Bots

Bots can be added to a team by every team member unless the setting is changed by either the Office 365 administrator or the team owner, as shown in Figure 7-4.

Note   External apps can be disabled by the Office 365 administrator. If you cannot add a bot, this could be the issue.

To add a bot to a team

1. Click the ellipse (...) to the right of the team that you want to add the bot to.

2. Click **Manage team**.

3. Click **Apps**.

4. Click the **Go to Store** button.

5. Click **bots** on the left underneath Store to show only the bot apps.

6. Select the bot to add to the team.

7. Select the team name from the **Add to team** drop-down menu, and then click **Install**.

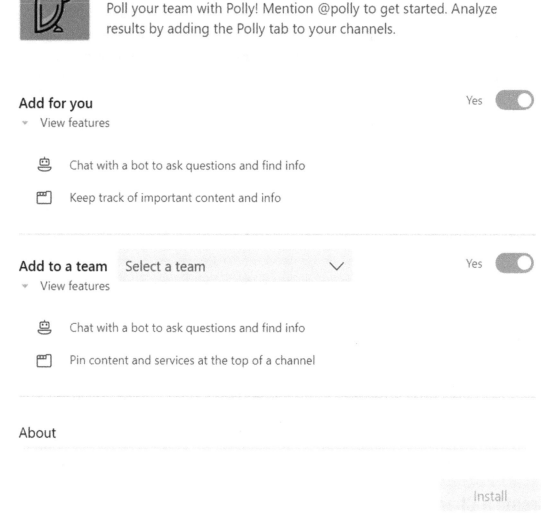

Figure 7-4. Installing a bot

Using Microsoft Flow with Teams

Microsoft Flow is a cloud-based application that is part of Office 365 and can be used for free as part of the same subscription with Microsoft Teams. Microsoft Flow is a business process automation tool that can collect data, automate approvals, copy files, send notifications, and more. Microsoft Flow can connect data from Microsoft Teams with data from other Office 365 applications, as well as third-party cloud-based applications.

For a flow to run, it needs to be triggered. There are many triggers that stem from hundreds of applications, but some examples are when an item in SharePoint is created or modified, when a new Microsoft Forms response is submitted, or when an Office 365 Outlook event is added, updated, or deleted. There are no Microsoft Teams triggers at this time, but Microsoft Flow functionality evolves often. Once a flow is triggered, conditions can be added that allow for different things to happen based on if they are true or not. Actions are tasks that the flow performs. Actions are what the flow does to complete the business process.

Teams Actions in Microsoft Flow

There are four actions that Microsoft Flow performs in Microsoft Teams, as shown in Figure 7-5. These actions provide an automatic way to create a channel, list the channels, list teams, and post messages.

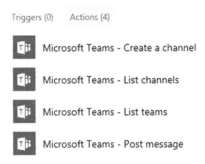

Figure 7-5. *Teams actions available in Microsoft Flow*

Create a Channel

The *create a channel* action in Microsoft Teams (see Figure 7-6) is extremely useful. This action automatically creates a channel based on a trigger. An attribute from a previous step can be used as the channel name; for example, you can create a flow that is triggered when an item is added to a SharePoint list. It then performs the action of creating a channel using the Title field from the SharePoint item as the channel name. A step can be added to the flow to only allow the creation a channel if someone in authority approves, such as the team owner or an IT professional.

Figure 7-6. *Creating a channel action in Microsoft Flow*

List Channels

The *list channels* action (see Figure 7-7) automatically provides a list of the channels in a team. It monitors channel creation; for example, an IT department could receive a weekly list of all channels to make sure that there aren't channels being created inappropriately. A condition can be added to the flow to only list channels that were created within a certain amount of days.

Figure 7-7. *List channels actions in Microsoft Flow*

List Teams

The *list teams* action (see Figure 7-8) is similar to the list channels action, except the teams are listed, not the channels. This is a great way to automate the process of monitoring the teams created in an Office 365 tenant. The team name, team ID, and team description attributes can be listed in an email or a report. Only the teams that the user running the flow is part of are listed.

Figure 7-8. *List teams action in Microsoft Flow*

121

Post a Message

The *post a message* action (see Figure 7-9) is likely the most commonly used Microsoft Teams action in Microsoft Flow. It notifies a team when something of interest has happened outside of Microsoft Teams. Common scenarios are to post a message to a team channel when a task in SharePoint is marked complete, when a new form is submitted, or when a bug is opened in Visual Studio Team Services.

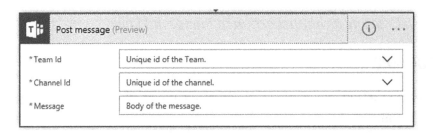

Figure 7-9. *Post message action in Microsoft Flow*

Templates

Microsoft Flow offers several prebuilt templates. There is very little configuration involved when using templates, and they are the easiest way to get started with using Microsoft Flow. As shown in Figure 7-10, you can search for teams, and then get a listing of all the templates that connect with Microsoft Teams. You need to have an account with any other service that the flow connects to, and you have to provide credentials for it to work. Microsoft Flow templates can act as a starting point, and then steps and conditions can be added.

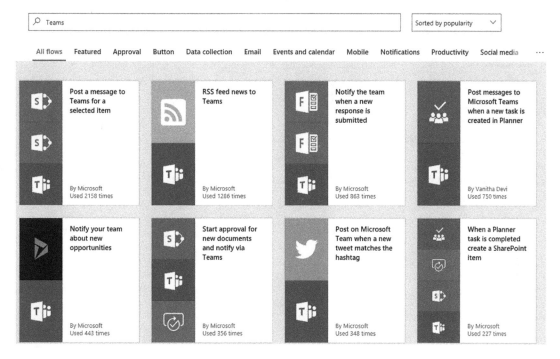

Figure 7-10. *Teams templates in Microsoft Flow*

Microsoft Flow App in Teams

The Microsoft Flow app, which can be installed in Microsoft Teams, provides a chat bot. This personal app helps users keep track of their flows. Flows can be created and edited within Teams. Since the Microsoft Flow app is a personal app, it is not seen by other team members. Each user installs the Microsoft Flow app themselves and can display their flows and approvals.

With the Microsoft Flow bot in Teams (see Figure 7-11), flows are run by command. When you chat with the Microsoft Flow bot, it lists the available flows to run. You can then command it to run a flow by typing **Run flow** followed by the number listed for the particular flow. At this time, only flows that run on a schedule are initiated by the Microsoft Flow bot. If you create a scheduled flow that lists all channels in a team and sends them in a monthly report, you can use the Microsoft Flow bot to send the report on demand as needed in Teams. Another scenario is if you have a scheduled flow that regularly posts articles, website links, or messages to social media sites such as LinkedIn or Twitter, you can use the Microsoft Flow bot to post on demand.

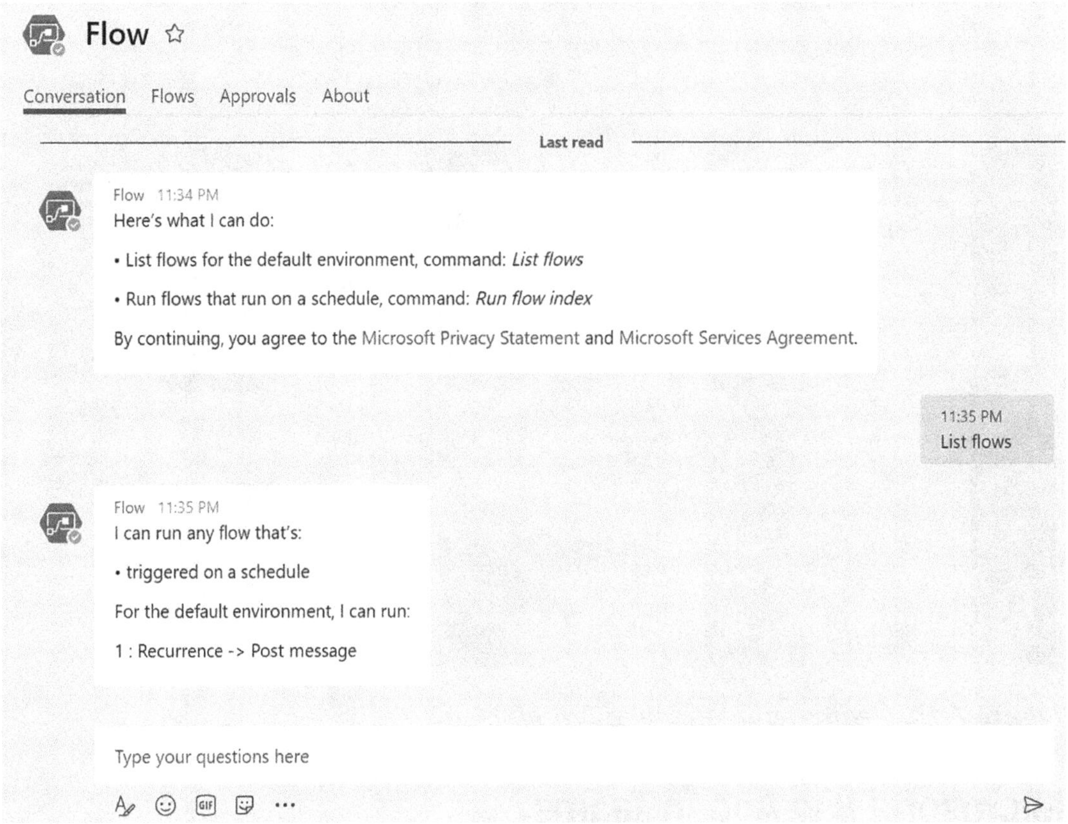

Flow ☆

Conversation   Flows   Approvals   About

———————————————————————— Last read ————————————————————————

Flow 11:34 PM
Here's what I can do:

• List flows for the default environment, command: *List flows*

• Run flows that run on a schedule, command: *Run flow index*

By continuing, you agree to the Microsoft Privacy Statement and Microsoft Services Agreement.

> 11:35 PM
> List flows

Flow 11:35 PM
I can run any flow that's:

• triggered on a schedule

For the default environment, I can run:

1 : Recurrence -> Post message

Type your questions here

A̲ ☺ GIF ☺ ...   ▷

Figure 7-11. *Microsoft Flow bot in Teams*

Summary

In this chapter, we reviewed the ways you can automate your business processes in Microsoft Teams using bots and Microsoft Flow. There are many benefits and time-saving opportunities with automating business processes in Microsoft Teams, but this is a more advanced aspect of the product that isn't always necessary. Focusing on users adopting the basic Microsoft Teams functionality is much more important. Be advised that although bots and flows are fairly new and exciting, they should not be set up if there is no business need. However, if you or a team member are spending a lot of time on an arduous task that is simple and repetitive, it is definitely worth exploring the business process automation options available within Microsoft Teams.

CHAPTER 8

Known Challenges and the Future

Some parts of Microsoft Teams are new and built with open source technologies, which is a different direction for Microsoft. Due to this (and other reasons), you will possibly find issues with the application when you use it. You will also most likely encounter some limitations in trying to accomplish your tasks as you work with it daily. Although this might sound a bit discouraging, Microsoft *is* investing in Microsoft Teams a great deal—more so than some of its other software. Depending on when you are reading this book (compared to when it was written), knowing the roadmap, issues, and user feedback can help make a realistic plan in how to use Microsoft Teams. In this chapter, we discuss issues that may occur when using Microsoft Teams.

Microsoft Teams replaces Skype for Business Online in Office 365 (it is not replacing Skype for Business On-Premises at the time of writing this book). Microsoft Teams has most of the Skype for Business Online functionality, but is missing some features. Additionally, Microsoft Teams is adding new video and calling features to the application beyond what Skype for Business provided.

Microsoft Teams is a new generation of collaboration software, in which the ability to work with others on files and conversations is provided. When you put these all together, you see that there are a myriad of different features coming to Microsoft Teams, but there are also some things that aren't quite working well at the onset.

Remember, Microsoft Teams is changing at a rapid pace, and depending on when you are reading this book, *some of the issues discussed in this chapter may have been fixed or have had work-arounds.*

© Melissa Hubbard, Matthew J. Bailey 2018
M. Hubbard and M. J. Bailey, *Mastering Microsoft Teams*, https://doi.org/10.1007/978-1-4842-3670-3_8

Issues with Working in Teams

In this section, we review some of the issues you might encounter while completing your work in Microsoft Teams.

Editing Office Documents

Let's say that you are writing a book and that you are consistently typing long paragraphs and pasting images into a Word document. The flow of how you work depends on how you created the Word document. As you can see in Figure 8-1, there are different ways to get a document in Teams.

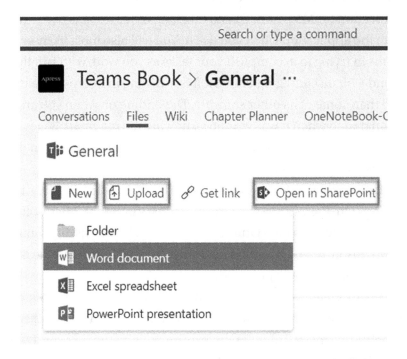

Figure 8-1. *The many ways to create or upload a document in Teams*

Microsoft has made a good deal of effort to create a seamless experience for users, so that working with Office files appears to be similar, regardless of how you access or create them. However, there are some features differ among methods. An example of this is when you create a Microsoft Teams Word document in a browser. This is really just embedding a Word Online authoring experience inside Microsoft Teams. Some people may not realize this. With Word Online, there is no ability to change the autosave timing. Word Online saves data as you type it. However, with the installed version of Word, you have the full set of Word configuration options.

The challenge is that creating a unified interface has good points and not-so-good points. If you are creating Word documents that are not very large, the online Word experience typically works well. For large documents, however, it is better to use the Word client by either opening the document in Word from Microsoft Teams or by creating a new file in Word and later uploading it to the files tab.

Importing and Exporting Channels, Data, and Files

A limitation of Microsoft Teams is its ability to move data, such as conversations between channels and/or other Teams. Additionally, moving groups of files to another team does not exist. If you plan properly, you can avoid a lot of issues involving the need to move the data around. However, as we explain in an upcoming section, the inability to secure channels differently from the team itself will cause people to organize them in different ways. This means that if you need to change how the team is organized and who sees what, you will not be able to move data and conversations to a new place. Because Microsoft does not make public all the plans for its software, it is unknown if the company is working on a tool to move these items.

Private Channels and Tabs

There is no option to secure items within a team to specific people, if you are in a team then you see everything in it (for the business version of the software, there is a separate version of Teams for educational institutions). This "all or nothing" concept can present challenges. As an example, let's say that you are creating a team to hire a candidate for an open position at your organization. You might place all the candidates' résumés on the team. You then invite everyone in Human Resources and the other hiring areas to the team. Each candidate could be interviewed and notes could be kept about the candidates to help determine which person is the final choice for the job.

The challenges start to appear when you need to restrict an area regarding the salary and the job offer to only people in Human Resources. There is no way to secure the offer details if it is in a channel or a tab. Also consider that in channels, the back end of Teams uses many different applications. The ability to secure all the content in these applications would take considerable implementation.

The good news is that we believe Microsoft is currently working on functionality to allow users to create private channels. We will have to wait and see if options for secure channels come and how they will operate.

Read-Only Permissions

There are at least two reasons for having a read-only team and one of them has been delivered just as this book was going to press. The first is for archival purposes. This *archive* option is now available in the "gear" icon at the bottom left of your Microsoft Teams interface.

The second reason, which is still unavailable when this book was being published, is to create an information-only team where users can only read information and only managers can post information. Although, you can change member permissions in team settings to only allow owners to post messages, this isn't exactly the same as a read-only team that is still in an active status.

Duplicate Team Names

One issue that could be confusing to your users is that Teams allows you to create teams with the same name, as seen in Figure 8-2. On the back end, the team is really a unique number called a GUID (globally unique identifier). The system uses this GUID to manage the team behind the scenes, so the duplicate name issue is not relevant to the system. The *display name* is what users see. As shown in Figure 8-2, multiple teams with the same name can confuse users who do not know which team is which.

Have an IT administrator or programmer create a script to prevent duplicate names, or purchase Azure Premium to take advantage of the groups naming policy feature to work around this issue.

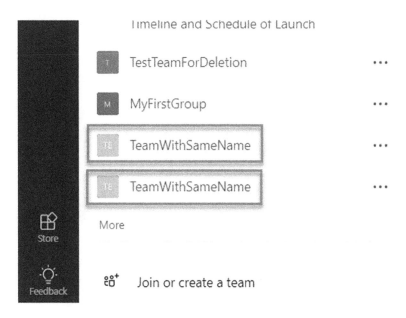

Figure 8-2. *Teams with the same display name can be created*

Deleting a Team Without Deleting the Group

When creating a new team, you have the option to use an existing Office 365 group, as shown in Figure 8-3. This is beneficial if your group members are certain that they want to use Teams as a replacement for Office 365 Groups. However, if users change their mind and decide they would like to go back to only using the original Office 365 group, there is an important issue. There is no way to disembark a group from a team. This means that if you delete the team, you also delete the pre-existing group with it.

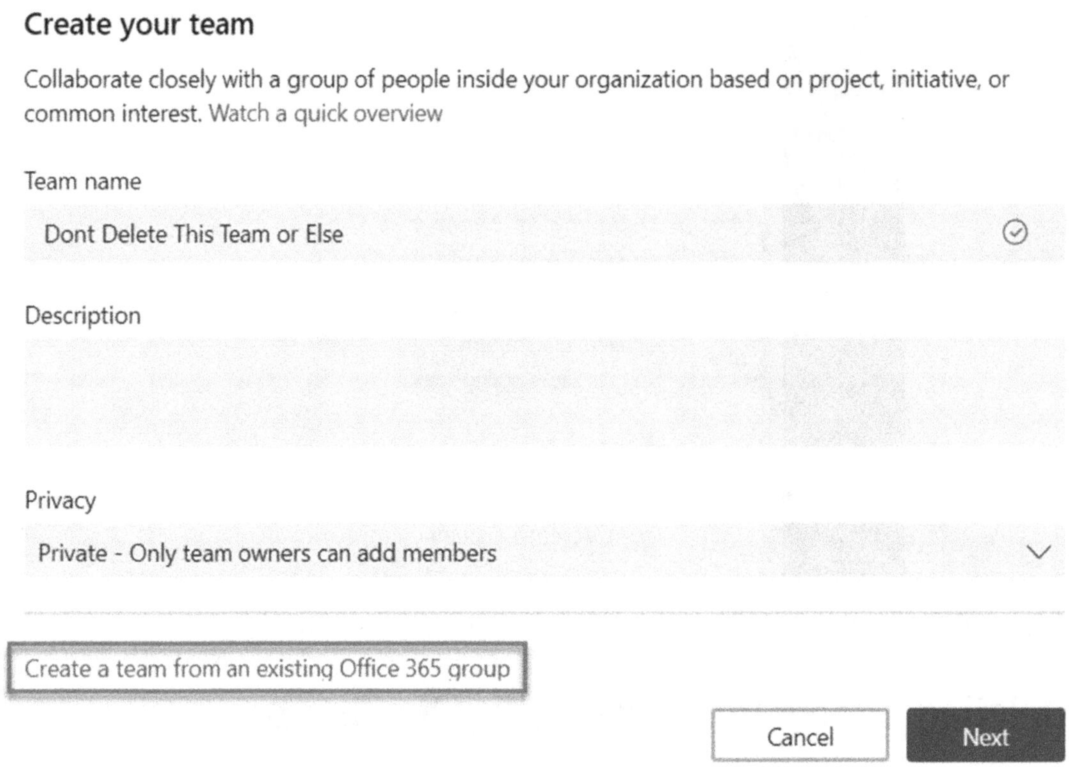

Create your team

Collaborate closely with a group of people inside your organization based on project, initiative, or common interest. Watch a quick overview

Team name

Dont Delete This Team or Else   ⊘

Description

Privacy

Private - Only team owners can add members   ⌄

Create a team from an existing Office 365 group

Cancel   Next

Figure 8-3. *The option to create a team from an existing Office 365 group*

Caution   There is no way to detach a group from a team at this time. Be certain that you want to convert your existing groups to teams.

Teams Can Be Slow

Microsoft Teams users need a solid Internet connection and a relatively powerful computer to use Teams successfully. Depending on what you are doing in Microsoft Teams, the amount of resources the Teams client uses can vary. It is important to note that Teams runs multiple processes at the same time. If you think about it, Teams is somewhat like trying to run Skype for Business, OneDrive for Business, Outlook, and any other application connected to it at the same time. Similar to Slack, it uses a lot of your computer's resources. For a comparison of how the Teams client works compared with Slack, see Figure 8-4. Microsoft is working on performance improvements, but what they are working on specifically and how much will improve are unknown at this time.

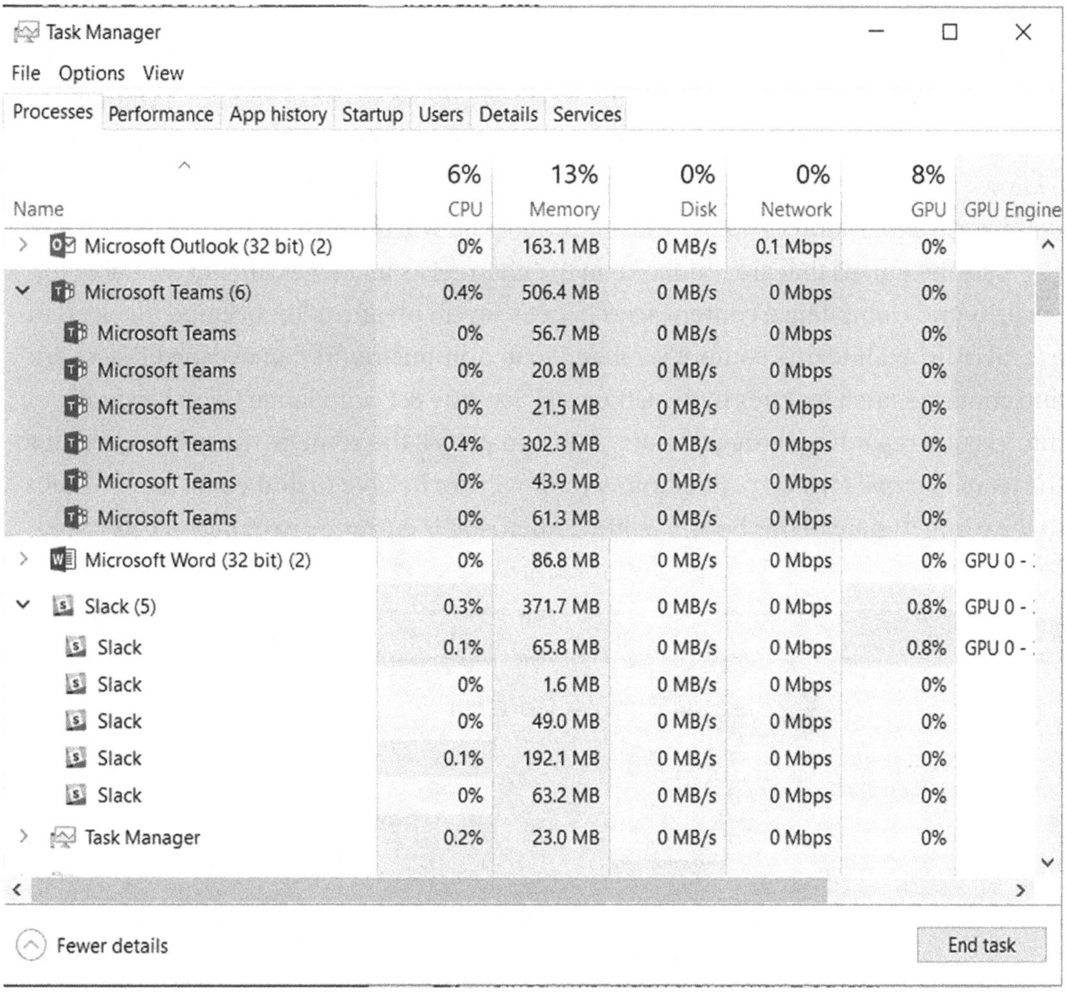

Figure 8-4. *The amount of memory Teams and Slack take up with no activity*

Issues with Communicating in Teams

Now let's move on to some the challenges you may face while communicating in Microsoft Teams.

Channel Email Addresses

As discussed earlier in the book, a channel comes with an email address to send to. This is great for making sure that an email is kept with the team and not a user's email box. If others are going to use this email address on a longer-term basis, the need for a simple and memorable email address might be of value. An example of an automatically created email address is seen in Figure 8-5. Unfortunately, the channel email address cannot be changed. Additionally, if you select *Remove email address* because you don't want others to email this channel, you cannot restore the email address at a later time. This could be a known issue or a feature that Microsoft is working to fix, but for now, it is best to not remove the email address unless you are certain you will not want to use the feature again.

Also, the emails that are rendered on the channel as messages are not available for Security and Compliance content search. Let's say an organization became involved in a legal issue, your team's content is related to it. Administrators can use the eDiscovery and content search features in the Office 365 Security & Compliance Center to find information regarding the legal issue. Unfortunately, if the content you need was sent to the team in email format, your administrator will not be able to find email content sent to the team. At time of this book's writing, Microsoft is currently working on this issue.

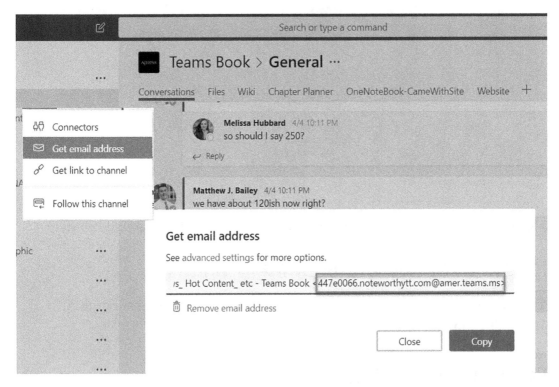

Figure 8-5. *A channel email address is pre-created by Teams for you*

Caution   Deleting a channel email address appears to be permanent; it is not recoverable.

Skype and Teams Interaction

Not all Skype for Business features are at parity with Microsoft Teams. It is possible that in some organizations, users have both Skype for Business (online or on-premises) and Microsoft Teams running simultaneously. An example of this is seen in Figure 8-6. Although Microsoft is currently working for feature parity between Microsoft Teams and Skype for Business Online/Skype for Business On-Premises, at the time of this book's writing, it was not available.

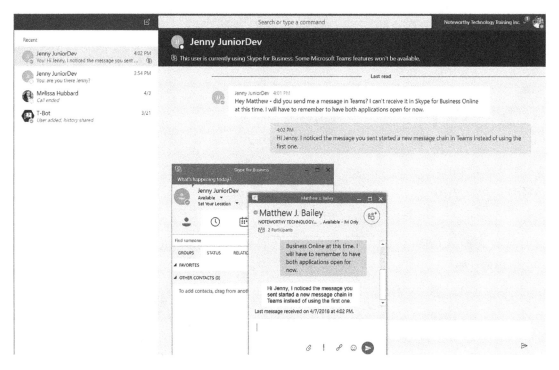

Figure 8-6. *Matthew's Teams interface and Jenny's Skype for Business Online chat box not staying in sync*

Caution   When users chat with different clients (one person has Skype for Business Online and one person is using Teams), not all of the features will work.

User Presence

There are a couple of issues with the user presence indicator. The first issue is related to the disconnect between Skype for Business and Microsoft Teams. As you can see in Figure 8-7, if a user is online in Skype for Business, it displays a green light that indicates their user presence. If a user is online using Microsoft Teams, however, the same does not apply. It is best to not rely on these indicators until full feature parity between Skype for Business and Microsoft Teams arrives.

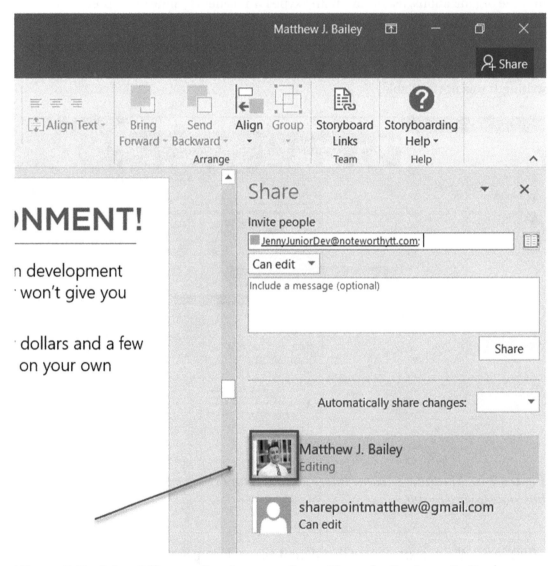

Figure 8-7. *Other Office applications can detect Skype for Business Online's user presence but not a Teams' user presence*

The other issue with Skype presence is that there are not any settings to change your presence in Microsoft Teams the way that there is in Skype for Business. With Skype for Business (as long as your administrator has not locked the field), you can change the length of time before your presence indicator turns to yellow, which signifies that you are away. In Microsoft Teams, you do not have this option, and as you can see in Figure 8-8, the presence indicator is not synched, thus giving the impression that you are not available when you actually are.

Figure 8-8. *Shows the presence indicator of Skype for Business and Teams not staying synchronized*

Bot Communications

As an end user, you may not be concerned with what you say to a bot, such as you see in Figure 8-9. As an administrator, you want to know that conversations between a user and a bot are not being recorded in the Office 365 Security & Compliance Center the way that user chats are. Neither are connection conversations. An end user may feel the effects of this issue if the administrator decides it makes Microsoft Teams incompliant with the governance policies in your organization.

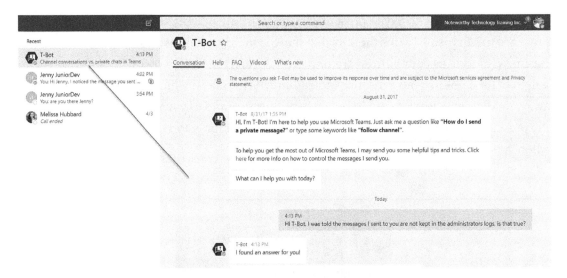

Figure 8-9. *Example of messages between a user and the T-Bot. These messages are not currently kept in the Office 365 Security & Compliance administration center. We were told that this is a bug Microsoft is looking into.*

Compact Chat Layout

Some users may only want to use the chat or IM functionality of Microsoft Teams. The issue here is that you cannot collapse the Microsoft Teams interface to a compact size comparable to that of other chat services. There has been feedback stating that some users only want the compact display of chats. Although you can shrink or minimize the Teams' application window size on your desktop, it won't be as small as a Skype for Business chat box, as seen in Figure 8-10. You have to scroll a bit to see an entire Teams chat. Microsoft is aware of this issue, and the company is currently working on improvements.

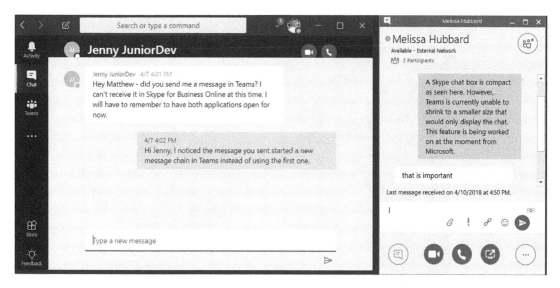

Figure 8-10. *Comparison of Teams minimized to the smallest setting compared to the existing Skype for Business chat box*

Issues with Meeting in Teams

There are a few known issues with meetings in Microsoft Teams, so let's quickly review them.

Calendar

If you create an Office 365 Group, you are most likely doing it from the Outlook interface. In Outlook, you have the option to control the calendar in a way that you would expect of the calendaring features from Microsoft. In Microsoft Teams, you are limited to a daily view that only goes out to the end of the current week. This means that users are not able to get a full picture of all the team events, which impacts planning deadlines and meetings. Although you could add the calendar in a tab via a web link to the Office 365 mailbox, it isn't as easy to understand with the calendar being so prevalent on the right side of the meetings area, such as seen in Figure 8-11. This feature request is currently under review by Microsoft.

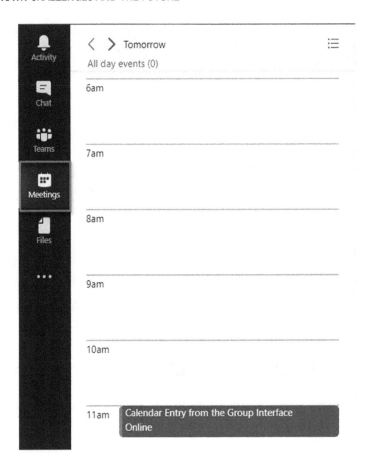

Figure 8-11. *An example of the Team calendar, which only has one view for the day and a limit of seeing the events past the end of the week*

Issues with Governing Teams

In this section, we review some known issues with governing Microsoft Teams.

Team Deletion

There is no way to prevent an owner from deleting their own team. This may or may not be a concern in your organization. As an alternative solution, as an Office 365 administrator, you can monitor teams being deleted. The administrator can place an alert in the Security & Compliance Center to send an email to a specific person if a team is deleted. The team is recoverable for 30 days after the date that it was deleted. Unfortunately, if you are an end user, you most likely do not have permission to the Office 365 admin center. You will need to ask for your team to be restored.

Caution   If preventing users in your organization from deleting a team is needed, consider asking an administrator to create a script that searches the soft deletion bin or to apply an audit log event alert.

Planned Roadmap

Microsoft is investing a great deal of money and effort into the Teams application. At time of writing, the planned addition of new features and capabilities is extensive, as shown in Table 1-1. Additionally, Microsoft is working on other features that are not listed here but are periodically released. The "continuous learning" concept greatly applies to Teams—for a few years at least. You can review the Teams' planned roadmap in Table 1-1.

Table 1-1. *Teams Features Expected to Be Released in 2018 by Microsoft (estimates, not guarantees)*

Feature	Early to Mid 2018	End-of-Year 2018
Teams templates		X
Messaging user-level policies	X	
Chat and conversation retention policies		X
Contact groups	X	
Unified presence	X	
Federated chat between teams and skype for business	X	
Import contacts from skype for business	X	
Skype for business interop with persistent chat	X	
Broadcast	X	
Cloud recording	X	
Federated meetings	X	
Large meeting support (~250)	X	
Lobby for PSTN callers	X	

(continued)

Table 1-1. (*continued*)

Feature	Early to Mid 2018	End-of-Year 2018
Outlook meeting schedule from other platforms (OWA, OLK, mobile)	X	
PowerPoint load and share	X	
Enable VTC interop services*	X	
Skype room systems support*	X	
Whiteboard and meeting notes	X	
Government version of teams	X	
Surface hub support	X	
1:1 to group call escalation with teams, skype for business, and PSTN participants	X	
Distinctive ring	X	
Boss and delegate support	X	
Call queues	X	
Do not disturb breakthrough	X	
Out of office support	X	
Call support between teams and skype consumers	X	
Hybrid connection to teams	X	
Australia, Japan, and Canada geolocations		X

User Feedback

Microsoft has taken on a new motto, "We're listening." We think that most of the time, Microsoft actually is. We personally feel that the company realizes that if it doesn't listen to its customers, who are paying for the products, it will eventually lose them. That said, a fair number of new features have come from user feedback on the UserVoice website at https://microsoftteams.uservoice.com/forums/555103-public (see Figure 8-12). Microsoft actively monitors user requests and responds on the site. Some requests are accepted, some are declined, some are investigated, and some are put on the backlog.

Although there is no guarantee that a request will be addressed, the more popular ones seem to receive some type of notation. In any case, take a look at the UserVoice website; you can voice your opinion or vote on an idea that is important to you.

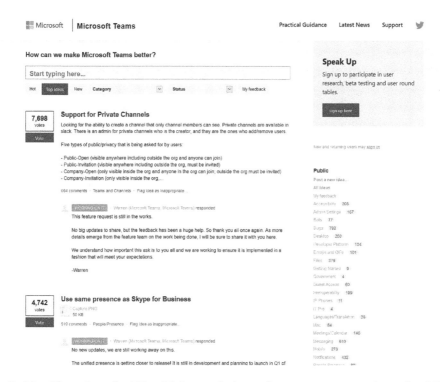

Figure 8-12. *Showing the UserVoice website, where new suggestions for Microsoft Teams are tracked between product users and Microsoft employees*

Summary

We have covered existing issues, user frustrations, and planned updates for Microsoft Teams in this chapter. Additionally, we provided an extensive end user guide to practical usage, collaboration, and governance within Microsoft Teams.

Microsoft Teams is one of the first applications that Microsoft released with the concept of an agile, continuous delivery concept. This means that we all have to keep our eyes open when using Microsoft Teams, as it will change often. By deciding to use Microsoft Teams, you have taken a step in the right direction toward transforming collaboration and communication with your teammates.

Index

© Melissa Hubbard, Matthew J. Bailey 2018
M. Hubbard and M. J. Bailey, *Mastering Microsoft Teams*, https://doi.org/10.1007/978-1-4842-3670-3

CPSIA information can be obtained
at www.ICGtesting.com
Printed in the USA
LVHW100138271020
669857LV00007B/559

9 781484 236697